THE

Year

OF

Mercy

~~~

INSPIRING WORDS
FROM

Pope
Francis

~~~

POPE FRANCIS

EDITED BY DIANE M. HOUDEK

Franciscan
MEDIA
Cincinnati, Ohio

Prayer of Pope Francis for the Jubilee ©Copyright Pontifical Council for
the Promotion of New Evangelization, Vatican State. All rights reserved.
Used by permission.
The Year of Mercy is published in collaboration with the Libreria Editrice
Vaticana. All excerpts © 2015, Libreria Editrice Vaticana
and used by permission.

Cover and book design by Mark Sullivan
Cover image © Giampiero Sposito | Reuters

Francis, Pope, 1936–
[Works. Selections. English]
A year of mercy : inspiring words from Pope Francis.
pages cm
ISBN 978-1-63253-082-0 (alk. paper)
1. Mercy. 2. Catholic Church—Doctrines. I. Title.
BV4647.M4F7313 2015
234'.5—dc23

2015034803

Published by Franciscan Media
28 W. Liberty St.
Cincinnati, OH 45202
www.FranciscanMedia.org

Printed in the United States of America.
Printed on acid-free paper.

15 16 17 18 19 5 4 3 2

Prayer of Pope Francis for the Jubilee

Lord Jesus Christ,

you have taught us to be merciful like the heavenly Father,

and have told us that whoever sees you sees Him.

Show us your face and we will be saved.

Your loving gaze freed Zacchaeus and Matthew from being enslaved by money;

the adulteress and Magdalene from seeking happiness only in created things;

made Peter weep after his betrayal,

and assured Paradise to the repentant thief.

Let us hear, as if addressed to each one of us, the words that you spoke to the Samaritan woman:

"If you knew the gift of God!"

You are the visible face of the invisible Father,

of the God who manifests his power above all by forgiveness and mercy:

let the Church be your visible face in the world, its Lord risen and glorified.

You willed that your ministers would also be clothed in weakness

in order that they may feel compassion for those in ignorance and error:

Introduction

~ Opening the Doors of Mercy ~

Dear brothers and sisters, I have often thought about how the Church might make clear its mission of being a witness to mercy. It is journey that begins with a spiritual conversion. For this reason, I have decided to call an *extraordinary Jubilee* that is to have the mercy of God at its center. It shall be a Holy Year of Mercy. We want to live this Year in the light of the Lord's words: "Be merciful, just as your Father is merciful" (cf. Lk 6:36).

—24 HOURS FOR THE LORD, ST PETER BASILICA,
FRIDAY, MARCH 13, 2015

From the very beginning of his pontificate, Pope Francis has made mercy his hallmark. It's no surprise, then, that he declared a special year dedicated to the contemplation of mercy. This is an extraordinary Jubilee Year beginning on December 8, 2015, the Solemnity of the Immaculate Conception, and ending on November 20, 2016, the Solemnity of Christ, King of the Universe.

We have a general understanding of a "jubilee" as a special anniversary, often in increments of decades. We speak of jubilee wedding anniversaries, often twenty-five or fifty years. The Old Testament concept of Jubilee is rooted in the Sabbath ritual, a time of rest and special blessings. The best description is found in the book of Leviticus:

> You shall count off seven weeks of years, seven times seven years, so that the period of seven weeks of years gives forty-nine years. Then you shall have the trumpet sounded loud; on the tenth day of the seventh month—on the day of atonement—you shall have the trumpet sounded throughout all your land. And you shall hallow the fiftieth year and you shall proclaim liberty throughout the land to all its inhabitants. It shall be a jubilee for you: you shall return, every one of you, to your property and every one of you to your family. That fiftieth year shall be a jubilee for you: you shall not sow, or reap the aftergrowth, or harvest the unpruned vines. For it is a jubilee; it shall be holy to you: you shall eat only what the field itself produces.

Many Catholics will remember the Great Jubilee declared by Pope St. John Paul II honoring the beginning of the third millennium since the birth of Christ. This continued a tradition in the Church begun in the Middle Ages. Jubilee years were declared through the centuries to mark special occasions, to encourage pilgrimage to Rome and other holy places, and to give people a way to find special blessings through God's forgiveness.

As the following pages will show, what's extraordinary about the Year of Mercy is that Pope Francis wants us to realize that God's mercy and grace surround us not just in special times and places but always and everywhere. This special year is a time to discover the extraordinary in the ordinary, to be surprised by God's mercy when we least expect it.

One of the interesting rituals of the Church's jubilee years is the opening of a special "Holy Door" at St. Peter's Basilica in Rome, at other major basilicas, and in cathedrals and even parish churches throughout the world. People were encouraged to go on pilgrimage to these holy places and to obtain special blessings by going through the Holy Doors into the church or cathedral. But Pope Francis makes it clear that we are called to cross the threshold of the church in the other direction as well, to go out into the world as missionaries, as evangelists, as signs of God's loving mercy in the world.

The reflections in this book are arranged to accompany you through this Jubilee Year of Mercy. Although not divided into days, weeks, and months, the chapters follow the liturgical year in a logical progression.

Beginning during the season of Advent, we reflect on the life of Jesus and the many ways he revealed the merciful face of God to all those whom he encountered.

At the beginning of the new year, we spend time with the Scriptures, especially the Gospels. The parables of mercy in Luke's Gospel, the psalms, the Beatitudes, and the last judgment parables in the Gospel of Matthew all give us inspired ways to understand the importance of divine mercy.

During Lent, we're encouraged to reflect on the concepts of judgment, justice, forgiveness, and mercy. Holy Week brings us to contemplation of the cross of Christ, a powerful meditation on the depths of divine mercy. We then celebrate the resurrection and Mary.

Through the long stretch of ordinary time, we reflect on the ways the Church becomes for us the place where we can encounter mercy. The sacraments, particularly the sacrament of reconciliation, are privileged moments of meeting our merciful God. When we know this mercy in our own lives, we are called to bring it to everyone we meet. This is the meaning of vocation.

Pope Francis is especially concerned about the way the mercy of God moves us toward unity and the painful divisions that still exist among faiths and within the various expressions of Christianity. He hopes that this Year of Mercy will move us toward healing those divisions through the grace of the Holy Spirit.

Finally, we come to a focus on the corporal and spiritual works of mercy. Beginning with the feasts of All Saints and All Souls and ending with the Solemnity of Christ the King, this final month of the Year of Mercy forcefully reminds us that works, not mere words, are the responsibility of every Christian.

As you reflect on these passages, let them challenge you to extend this Year of Mercy into a lifetime of following Jesus Christ and being merciful as the Father is merciful.

—*Diane M. Houdek,*
editor

CHAPTER ONE

~ Crossing the Threshold of Mercy ~

A LIVING SIGN OF THE FATHER'S LOVE IN THE WORLD

I have chosen the date of 8 December because of its rich meaning in the recent history of the Church. In fact, I will open the Holy Door on the fiftieth anniversary of the closing of the Second Vatican Ecumenical Council. The Church feels a great need to keep this event alive. With the Council, the Church entered a new phase of her history. The Council Fathers strongly perceived, as a true breath of the Holy Spirit, a need to talk about God to men and women of their time in a more accessible way. The walls which for too long had made the Church a kind of fortress were torn down and the time had come to proclaim the Gospel in a new way. It was a new phase of the same evangelization that had existed from the beginning. It was a fresh undertaking for all Christians to bear witness to their faith with greater enthusiasm and conviction. The Church sensed a responsibility to be a living sign of the Father's love in the world.

MISERICORDIAE VULTUS, BULL OF INDICTION OF THE
EXTRAORDINARY JUBILEE YEAR OF MERCY, 4

CONTEMPLATING THE FACE OF MERCY

With these sentiments of gratitude for everything the Church has received, and with a sense of responsibility for the task that lies ahead, we shall cross the threshold of the Holy Door fully confident that the strength of the Risen Lord, who constantly supports us on our pilgrim way, will sustain us. May the Holy Spirit, who guides the steps of believers in cooperating with the work of salvation wrought by Christ, lead the way and support the People of God so that they may contemplate the face of mercy [cf. Second Vatican Ecumenical Council, Dogmatic Constitution on the Church, *Lumen Gentium*, 16: Pastoral Constitution on the Church in the Modern World, *Gaudium et Spes*, 15].

MISERICORDIAE VULTUS, BULL OF INDICTION OF THE
EXTRAORDINARY JUBILEE YEAR OF MERCY, 4

A Year Steeped in Mercy

We will entrust the life of the Church, all humanity, and the entire cosmos to the Lordship of Christ, asking him to pour out his mercy upon us like the morning dew, so that everyone may work together to build a brighter future. How much I desire that the year to come will be steeped in mercy, so that we can go out to every man and woman, bringing the goodness and tenderness of God! May the balm of mercy reach everyone, both believers and those far away, as a sign that the Kingdom of God is already present in our midst!

MISERICORDIAE VULTUS, BULL OF INDICTION OF THE
EXTRAORDINARY JUBILEE YEAR OF MERCY, 5

GOD IS EVER PATIENT AND MERCIFUL

"It is proper to God to exercise mercy, and he manifests his omnipotence particularly in this way" [Summa Theologiae, II–II, q. 30. a. 4.]. Saint Thomas Aquinas' words show that God's mercy, rather than a sign of weakness, is the mark of his omnipotence. For this reason the liturgy, in one of its most ancient collects, has us pray: "O God, who reveal your power above all in your mercy and forgiveness"… Throughout the history of humanity, God will always be the One who is present, close, provident, holy, and merciful.

"Patient and merciful." These words often go together in the Old Testament to describe God's nature. His being merciful is concretely demonstrated in his many actions throughout the history of salvation where his goodness prevails over punishment and destruction.

MISERICORDIAE VULTUS, BULL OF INDICTION OF THE
EXTRAORDINARY JUBILEE YEAR OF MERCY, 6

THE FATHER ALWAYS PARDONS

Let us not forget this word: God never ever tires of forgiving us! "Well, Father what is the problem?" Well, the problem is that we ourselves tire, we do not want to ask, we grow weary of asking for forgiveness. He never tires of forgiving, but at times we get tired of asking for forgiveness. Let us never tire, let us never tire! He is the loving Father who always pardons, who has that heart of mercy for us all. And let us too learn to be merciful to everyone. Let us invoke the intercession of Our Lady who held in her arms the Mercy of God made man.

ANGELUS, ST. PETER'S SQUARE
SUNDAY, MARCH 17, 2013

Focus on the Heart

The call of Jesus pushes each of us never to stop at the surface of things, especially when we are dealing with a person. We are called to look beyond, to focus on the heart to see [of] how much generosity everyone is capable. No one can be excluded from the mercy of God; everyone knows the way to access it and the Church is *the house that welcomes all and refuses no one*. Its doors remain wide open, so that those who are touched by grace can find the certainty of forgiveness. The greater the sin, so much the greater must be the love that the Church expresses toward those who convert.

24 HOURS FOR THE LORD, ST. PETER'S BASILICA
FRIDAY, MARCH 13, 2015

God Forgives with a Caress

We look at the sky, the many stars, but when the morning sun comes, we don't see the stars. Such is the mercy of God: it is a great light of love, of tenderness. God doesn't forgive with a decree but with a caress. He forgives by caressing the wounds caused by our sins, because he is involved in forgiveness, is involved in our salvation.

MORNING MEDITATION IN THE CHAPEL OF THE
DOMUS SANCTAE MARTHAE
MONDAY, APRIL 7, 2014

Unceasing Patience

God's face is the face of a merciful father who is always patient. Have you thought about God's patience, the patience he has with each one of us? That is his mercy. He always has patience, patience with us, he understands us, he waits for us, he does not tire of forgiving us if we are able to return to him with a contrite heart. "Great is God's mercy," says the Psalm. A little mercy makes the world less cold and more just. We need to understand properly this mercy of God, this merciful Father who is so patient.

ANGELUS, ST. PETER'S SQUARE
SUNDAY, MARCH 17, 2013

Mercy Holds the World in Existence

I remember, when I had only just become a bishop in the year 1992, an elderly woman approached me, humble, very humble, and over eighty years old. I looked at her, and I said, "Grandmother"—because in our country that is how we address the elderly—do you want to make your confession?" "Yes," she said to me. "But if you have not sinned...." And she said to me: "We all have sins...." "But perhaps the Lord does not forgive them." "The Lord forgives all things," she said to me with conviction. "But how do you know, Madam?" "If the Lord did not forgive everything, the world would not exist." I felt an urge to ask her: "Tell me, Madam, did you study at the Gregorian [University]?" because that is the wisdom which the Holy Spirit gives: inner wisdom focused on God's mercy.

ANGELUS, ST. PETER'S SQUARE
SUNDAY, MARCH 17, 2013

THE BRIDGE THAT CONNECTS US TO GOD

We need constantly to contemplate the mystery of mercy. It is a wellspring of joy, serenity, and peace. Our salvation depends on it. Mercy: the word reveals the very mystery of the Most Holy Trinity. Mercy: the ultimate and supreme act by which God comes to meet us. Mercy: the fundamental law that dwells in the heart of every person who looks sincerely into the eyes of his brothers and sisters on the path of life. Mercy: the bridge that connects God and man, opening our hearts to the hope of being loved forever despite our sinfulness.

MISERICORDIAE VULTUS, BULL OF INDICTION OF THE
EXTRAORDINARY JUBILEE YEAR OF MERCY, 2

Proof of God's Love

Merciful like the Father, therefore, is the "motto" of this Holy Year. In mercy, we find proof of how God loves us. He gives his entire self, always, freely, asking nothing in return. He comes to our aid whenever we call upon him. What a beautiful thing that the Church begins her daily prayer with the words, "O God, come to my assistance. O Lord, make haste to help me" (Ps 70:2)! The assistance we ask for is already the first step of God's mercy toward us. He comes to assist us in our weakness. And his help consists in helping us accept his presence and closeness to us. Day after day, touched by his compassion, we also can become compassionate towards others.

MISERICORDIAE VULTUS, BULL OF INDICTION OF THE EXTRAORDINARY JUBILEE YEAR OF MERCY, 13

THE JOURNEY OF LIFE

The practice of pilgrimage has a special place in the Holy Year, because it represents the journey each of us makes in this life. Life itself is a pilgrimage, and the human being is a viator, a pilgrim travelling along the road, making his way to the desired destination. Similarly, to reach the Holy Door in Rome or in any other place in the world, everyone, each according to his or her ability, will have to make a pilgrimage. This will be a sign that mercy is also a goal to reach and requires dedication and sacrifice. May pilgrimage be an impetus to conversion: by crossing the threshold of the Holy Door, we will find the strength to embrace God's mercy and dedicate ourselves to being merciful with others as the Father has been with us.

MISERICORDIAE VULTUS, BULL OF INDICTION OF THE EXTRAORDINARY JUBILEE YEAR OF MERCY, 14

A Year of the Lord's Favor

"The Spirit of the Lord God is upon me, because the Lord has anointed me to bring good tidings to the afflicted; he has sent me to bind up the brokenhearted, to proclaim liberty to the captives, and freedom to those in captivity; to proclaim the year of the Lord's favor" (Is 61:1–2). A "year of the Lord's favor" or "mercy": this is what the Lord proclaimed and this is what we wish to live now. This Holy Year will bring to the fore the richness of Jesus' mission echoed in the words of the prophet: to bring a word and gesture of consolation to the poor, to proclaim liberty to those bound by new forms of slavery in modern society, to restore sight to those who can see no more because they are caught up in themselves, to restore dignity to all those from whom it has been robbed. The preaching of Jesus is made visible once more in the response of faith which Christians are called to offer by their witness. May the words of the Apostle accompany us: he who does acts of mercy, let him do them with cheerfulness (cf. Rom 12:8).

MISERICORDIAE VULTUS, BULL OF INDICTION OF THE EXTRAORDINARY JUBILEE YEAR OF MERCY, 16

CHAPTER TWO

~ Jesus, the Face of Mercy ~

Everything in Jesus Speaks of Mercy

With our eyes fixed on Jesus and his merciful gaze, we experience the love of the Most Holy Trinity. The mission Jesus received from the Father was that of revealing the mystery of divine love in its fullness. "God is love" (1 Jn 4:8,16), John affirms for the first and only time in all of Holy Scripture. This love has now been made visible and tangible in Jesus' entire life. His person is nothing but love, a love given gratuitously. The relationships he forms with the people who approach him manifest something entirely unique and unrepeatable. The signs he works, especially in favor of sinners, the poor, the marginalized, the sick, and the suffering, are all meant to teach mercy. Everything in him speaks of mercy. Nothing in him is devoid of compassion.

MISERICORDIAE VULTUS, BULL OF INDICTION OF THE
EXTRAORDINARY JUBILEE YEAR OF MERCY, 8

Jesus Is God's Heart

We do not believe in an ethereal God, we believe in a God who became flesh, who has a heart and this heart today speaks to us thus: "Come to me. If you are tired, oppressed and I will give you rest. But the smallest, treat them with compassion, with the same tenderness with which I treat you." The Heart of Jesus Christ says this to us today.

BASILICA OF ST. JOHN LATERAN
FRIDAY, JUNE 12, 2015

THE HEAVENS OPEN WITH THE BIRTH OF JESUS

The manifestation of the Son of God on earth marks the beginning of the great time of mercy, after sin had closed the heavens, raising itself as a barrier between the human being and his Creator. With the birth of Jesus the heavens open! God gives us in Christ the guarantee of an indestructible love. From the moment the Word became flesh it is therefore possible to see the open heavens. It was possible for the shepherds of Bethlehem, for the Magi of the East, for the Baptist, for Jesus' Apostles, and for St. Stephen, the first martyr, who exclaimed: "Behold, I see the heavens opened!" (Acts 7:56). And it is possible for each one of us, if we allow ourselves to be suffused with God's love, which is given to us for the first time in Baptism by means of the Holy Spirit. Let us allow ourselves to be invaded by God's love! This is the great time of mercy! Do not forget it: this is the great time of Mercy!

ANGELUS, ST. PETER'S SQUARE
SUNDAY, JANUARY 12, 2014

SHOWING MERCY TO SINNERS

I think we too are the people who, on the one hand want to listen to Jesus, but on the other hand, at times, like to find a stick to beat others with, to condemn others. And Jesus has this message for us: mercy. I think—and I say it with humility—that this is the Lord's most powerful message: mercy. It was he himself who said: "I did not come for the righteous." The righteous justify themselves. Go on, then, even if you can do it, I cannot! But they believe they can. "I came for sinners" (Mk 2:17).

HOMILY, THE PARISH OF ST. ANNA IN THE VATICAN
FIFTH SUNDAY OF LENT, MARCH 17, 2013

EVERY ENCOUNTER WITH JESUS CHANGES OUR LIVES

The Lord is greater than prejudice, which is why he was not afraid to address the Samaritan woman: mercy is greater than prejudice. We must learn this well! Mercy is greater than prejudice, and Jesus is so very merciful, very! The outcome of that encounter by the well was the woman's transformation: "the woman left her water jar" [John 4:28], with which she had come to draw water, and ran to the city to tell people about her extraordinary experience. In this Gospel passage we likewise find the impetus to "leave behind our water jar," the symbol of everything that is seemingly important, but loses all its value before the "love of God." We all have one, or more than one! I ask you, and myself: "What is your interior water jar, the one that weighs you down, that distances you from God?"

ANGELUS, ST. PETER'S SQUARE
THIRD SUNDAY OF LENT, MARCH 23, 2014

Like Sheep without a Shepherd

Jesus, seeing the crowds of people who followed him, realized that they were tired and exhausted, lost and without a guide, and he felt deep compassion for them (cf. Mt 9:36). On the basis of this compassionate love he healed the sick who were presented to him (cf. Mt 14:14), and with just a few loaves of bread and fish he satisfied the enormous crowd (cf. Mt 15:37). What moved Jesus in all of these situations was nothing other than mercy, with which he read the hearts of those he encountered and responded to their deepest need.

MISERICORDIAE VULTUS, BULL OF INDICTION OF THE EXTRAORDINARY JUBILEE YEAR OF MERCY, 8

What Mercy Awakens within Us

Jesus looks at Matthew and awakens something new within him, something that he did not know. The gaze of Jesus makes him feel an interior wonder, and makes him hear the call of Jesus: follow me. It only took a moment to understand that that look had changed his life forever. And it is in this moment that Matthew says yes, leaves everything and goes with the Lord.

DAILY MEDITATION, DOMUS SANCTAE MARTHAE
FRIDAY, JULY 5, 2013

The Memory of Mercy Propels Us Forward

The first moment of the encounter, which consists of a deep spiritual experience is followed by a second experience: that of celebration. The Gospel continues with Jesus sitting at table with publicans and sinners; those who were rejected by society. This is the contradiction of the celebration of God: the Lord feasts with sinners. The encounter with Jesus and the mercy of God should be celebrated. But life is not one big party. There is a time for celebration, but then there must be daily work, fuelled by the memory of that first encounter. It is the memory of mercy and of that celebration that gives Matthew, and everyone who has chosen to follow Christ, the strength to go forward. This must be remembered forever.

DAILY MEDITATION, DOMUS SANCTAE MARTHAE
FRIDAY, JULY 5, 2013

THE CERTAINTY THAT WE ARE FORGIVEN

Luke 7:36–50 opens for us a path of hope and comfort.

There is the love of the sinful woman, who humbles herself before the Lord; but first there is the merciful love of Jesus for her, which pushes her to approach. Her cry of repentance and joy washes the feet of the Master, and her hair dries them with gratitude; her kisses are pure expression of her affection; and the fragrant ointment poured out with abundance attests how precious He is to her eyes. This woman's every gesture speaks of love and expresses her desire to have an unshakeable certainty in her life: that of being forgiven. And Jesus gives this assurance: welcoming her, He demonstrates God's love for her, just for her! For her, a new season now begins; she is reborn in love, to a new life.

24 HOURS FOR THE LORD, ST. PETER'S BASILICA
FRIDAY, MARCH 13, 2015

CHAPTER THREE

~ Mercy in Scripture: Only Say the Word ~

God's Mercy Is Shown in Loving Concern

As we can see in Sacred Scripture, mercy is a key word that indicates God's action towards us. He does not limit himself merely to affirming his love, but makes it visible and tangible. Love, after all, can never be just an abstraction. By its very nature, it indicates something concrete: intentions, attitudes, and behaviors that are shown in daily living. The mercy of God is his loving concern for each one of us. He feels responsible; that is, he desires our well-being and he wants to see us happy, full of joy, and peaceful. This is the path which the merciful love of Christians must also travel. As the Father loves, so do his children. Just as he is merciful, so we are called to be merciful to each other.

MISERICORDIAE VULTUS, BULL OF INDICTION OF THE
EXTRAORDINARY JUBILEE YEAR OF MERCY, 9

Mercy Is Central to the Gospel

In the Gospel the essential thing is mercy. God sent his Son, God made himself man in order to save us, that is, in order to grant us his mercy. Jesus says this clearly, summarizing his teaching for the disciples: "Be merciful, even as your Father is merciful" (Lk 6:36). Can there be a Christian who isn't merciful? No. A Christian must necessarily be merciful, because this is the center of the Gospel. And faithful to this teaching, the Church can only repeat the same thing to her children: "Be merciful," as the Father is, and as Jesus was. Mercy.

GENERAL AUDIENCE, ST. PETER'S SQUARE,
WEDNESDAY, SEPTEMBER 10, 2014

What Is God Saying to Me?

One should truly listen to the word, in the Bible, in the Gospel, meditating on the Scriptures to put their content into practice every day. But to scan the Gospel superficially is not listening to the Word of God: this is reading the Word of God, as if one would read a comic strip. To listen to God's Word is to read it and ask oneself: "What does this say to my heart?" Only in this way, in fact, does our life change. This happens every time we open the Gospel and read a passage and ask ourselves: 'Is God speaking to me with this, is he saying something to me'?" This means to listen to the Word of God, to listen with the ears and listen with the heart, to open the heart to God's Word.

MORNING MEDITATION IN THE CHAPEL OF THE
DOMUS SANCTAE MARTHAE,
TUESDAY, SEPTEMBER 23, 2014

A FATHER WHO NEVER GIVES UP

In the parables devoted to mercy, Jesus reveals the nature of God as that of a Father who never gives up until he has forgiven the wrong and overcome rejection with compassion and mercy. We know these parables well, three in particular: the lost sheep, the lost coin, and the father with two sons (cf. Lk 15:1–32). In these parables, God is always presented as full of joy, especially when he pardons. In them we find the core of the Gospel and of our faith, because mercy is presented as a force that overcomes everything, filling the heart with love and bringing consolation through pardon.

MISERICORDIAE VULTUS, BULL OF INDICTION OF THE
EXTRAORDINARY JUBILEE YEAR OF MERCY, 9

Only Love Fills the Void

Chapter 15 of the Gospel of Luke contains three parables of mercy: the lost sheep, the lost coin, and then the longest of them, characteristic of St. Luke, the parable of the father of two sons, the "prodigal" son and the son who believes he is "righteous," who believes he is saintly. All three of these parables speak of the joy of God. God is joyful. This is interesting: God is joyful! And what is the joy of God? The joy of God is forgiving, the joy of God is forgiving! The joy of a shepherd who finds his little lamb; the joy of a woman who finds her coin; it is the joy of a father welcoming home the son who was lost, who was as though dead and has come back to life, who has come home. Here is the entire Gospel! Here! The whole Gospel, all of Christianity, is here! But make sure that it is not sentiment, it is not being a "do-gooder"! On the contrary, mercy is the true force that can save man and the world from the "cancer" that is sin, moral evil, spiritual evil. Only love fills the void, the negative chasms that evil opens in hearts and in history. Only love can do this, and this is God's joy!

ANGELUS, ST. PETER'S SQUARE
SUNDAY, SEPTEMBER 15, 2013

Each of Us Is Lost in Some Way

Jesus is all mercy, Jesus is all love: he is God made man. Each of us, each one of us, is that little lost lamb, the coin that was mislaid; each one of us is that son who has squandered his freedom on false idols, illusions of happiness, and has lost everything. But God does not forget us, the Father never abandons us. He is a patient father, always waiting for us! He respects our freedom, but he remains faithful forever. And when we come back to him, he welcomes us like children into his house, for he never ceases, not for one instant, to wait for us with love. And his heart rejoices over every child who returns. He is celebrating because he is joy. God has this joy, when one of us sinners goes to him and asks his forgiveness.

ANGELUS, ST. PETER'S SQUARE
SUNDAY, SEPTEMBER 15, 2013

Do We Have Mercy and Forgiveness in Our Hearts? What is the danger? It is that we presume we are righteous and judge others. We also judge God, because we think that he should punish sinners, condemn them to death, instead of forgiving. So 'yes' then we risk staying outside the Father's house! Like the older brother in the parable, who rather than being content that his brother has returned, grows angry with the father who welcomes him and celebrates. If in our heart there is no mercy, no joy of forgiveness, we are not in communion with God, even if we observe all of his precepts, for it·is love that saves, not the practice of precepts alone. It is love of God and neighbor that brings fulfillment to all the Commandments. And this is the love of God, his joy: forgiveness. He waits for us always! Maybe someone has some heaviness in his heart: "But, I did this, I did that...." He expects you! He is your father: he waits for you always!

ANGELUS, ST. PETER'S SQUARE
SUNDAY, SEPTEMBER 15, 2013

God Is Always Waiting for Us

The courage to trust in Jesus' mercy, to trust in his patience, to seek refuge always in the wounds of his love. Maybe someone among us here is thinking: my sin is so great, I am as far from God as the younger son in the parable, my unbelief is like that of Thomas; I don't have the courage to go back, to believe that God can welcome me and that he is waiting for me, of all people. But God is indeed waiting for you; he asks of you only the courage to go to him. How many times in my pastoral ministry have I heard it said: "Father, I have many sins"; and I have always pleaded: "Don't be afraid, go to him, he is waiting for you, he will take care of everything." We hear many offers from the world around us; but let us take up God's offer instead: his is a caress of love. For God, we are not numbers, we are important, indeed we are the most important thing to him; even if we are sinners, we are what is closest to his heart.

BASILICA OF ST. JOHN LATERAN
SECOND SUNDAY OF EASTER—DIVINE MERCY SUNDAY
APRIL 7, 2013

MERCIFUL ACTS REVEAL GOD'S TRUE CHILDREN

From another parable, we cull an important teaching for our Christian lives. In reply to Peter's question about how many times it is necessary to forgive, Jesus says: "I do not say seven times, but seventy times seven times" (Mt 18:22). He then goes on to tell the parable of the "ruthless servant," who, called by his master to return a huge amount, begs him on his knees for mercy. His master cancels his debt. But he then meets a fellow servant who owes him a few cents and who in turn begs on his knees for mercy, but the first servant refuses his request and throws him into jail. When the master hears of the matter, he becomes infuriated and, summoning the first servant back to him, says, "Should not you have had mercy on your fellow servant, as I had mercy on you?" (Mt 18:33). Jesus concludes, "So also my heavenly Father will do to every one of you, if you do not forgive your brother from your heart" (Mt 18:35). This parable contains a profound teaching for all of us. Jesus affirms that mercy is not only an action of the Father, it becomes a criterion for ascertaining who his true children are. In short, we are called to show mercy because mercy has first been shown to us.

MISERICORDIAE VULTUS, BULL OF INDICTION OF THE
EXTRAORDINARY JUBILEE YEAR OF MERCY, 9

WE ARE CALLED TO FORGIVE
AS WE HAVE BEEN FORGIVEN

Pardoning offenses becomes the clearest expression of merciful love, and for us Christians it is an imperative from which we cannot excuse ourselves. At times how hard it seems to forgive! And yet pardon is the instrument placed into our fragile hands to attain serenity of heart. To let go of anger, wrath, violence, and revenge are necessary conditions to living joyfully. Let us therefore heed the Apostle's exhortation: "Do not let the sun go down on your anger" (Eph 4:26). Above all, let us listen to the words of Jesus who made mercy an ideal of life and a criterion for the credibility of our faith: "Blessed are the merciful, for they shall obtain mercy" (Mt 5:7): the beatitude to which we should particularly aspire in this Holy Year.

MISERICORDIAE VULTUS, BULL OF INDICTION OF THE
EXTRAORDINARY JUBILEE YEAR OF MERCY, 9

THE BEATITUDES ARE THE CHRISTIAN'S IDENTITY CARD
When someone asks, "How does one become a good Christian?" the answer is simple: do what Jesus says in his discourse on the Beatitudes. The Lord knows sin and grace, and he knows the paths that lead to sin and to grace. "Blessed are the merciful, for they will find mercy." This refers to those who forgive, who understand others' mistakes. Jesus doesn't say, "Blessed are those who seek vengeance," or who say "an eye for an eye, a tooth for a tooth," but he calls blessed those who forgive, the merciful. It's always important to think that we are all an army of forgiven! All of us have been forgiven! And this is why he who takes this path of forgiveness is blessed.

MORNING MEDITATION IN THE CHAPEL OF THE
DOMUS SANCTAE MARTHAE
MONDAY, JUNE 9, 2014

GOD'S MERCY ENDURES FOREVER

"For his mercy endures forever." This is the refrain that repeats after each verse in Psalm 136 as it narrates the history of God's revelation. By virtue of mercy, all the events of the Old Testament are replete with profound salvific import. Mercy renders God's history with Israel a history of salvation. To repeat continually "for his mercy endures forever," as the psalm does, seems to break through the dimensions of space and time, inserting everything into the eternal mystery of love. It is as if to say that not only in history, but for all eternity man will always be under the merciful gaze of the Father.

MISERICORDIAE VULTUS, BULL OF INDICTION OF THE
EXTRAORDINARY JUBILEE YEAR OF MERCY, 7

God's Mercy Reveals Deep Love

Here are some other expressions of the Psalmist: "He heals the brokenhearted, and binds up their wounds.... The Lord lifts up the downtrodden, he casts the wicked to the ground" (Ps 147:3, 6). In short, the mercy of God is not an abstract idea, but a concrete reality with which he reveals his love as of that of a father or a mother, moved to the very depths out of love for their child. It is hardly an exaggeration to say that this is a "visceral" love. It gushes forth from the depths naturally, full of tenderness and compassion, indulgence and mercy.

MISERICORDIAE VULTUS, BULL OF INDICTION OF THE EXTRAORDINARY JUBILEE YEAR OF MERCY, 6

Chapter Four

~ Not Judgment but Forgiveness:

The Light of Mercy ~

As the Father Is Merciful

We want to live this Jubilee Year in light of the Lord's words: Merciful like the Father. The Evangelist reminds us of the teaching of Jesus who says, "Be merciful just as your Father is merciful" (Lk 6:36). It is a program of life as demanding as it is rich with joy and peace. Jesus's command is directed to anyone willing to listen to his voice (cf. Lk 6:27). In order to be capable of mercy, therefore, we must first of all dispose ourselves to listen to the Word of God. This means rediscovering the value of silence in order to meditate on the Word that comes to us. In this way, it will be possible to contemplate God's mercy and adopt it as our lifestyle.

MISERICORDIAE VULTUS, BULL OF INDICTION OF THE
EXTRAORDINARY JUBILEE YEAR OF MERCY, 13

LOVE GOES BEYOND JUSTICE

This woman has really met the Lord. In silence, she opened her heart to Him; in pain, she showed repentance for her sins; with her tears, she appealed to the goodness of God for forgiveness. For her, there will be no judgment except that which comes from God, and this is the judgment of mercy. The protagonist of this meeting is certainly the love that goes beyond justice. Simon the Pharisee, on the contrary, *cannot find the path of love*. He stands firm upon the threshold of formality. He is not capable of taking the next step to go meet Jesus, who brings him salvation. Simon limited himself to inviting Jesus to dinner, but did not really welcome Him. In his thoughts, he invokes only justice, and in so doing, he errs. *His judgment on the woman distances him from the truth* and does not allow him even to understand who [his] guest is. He stopped at the surface, he was not able to look to the heart. Before Jesus' parable and the question of which a servant would love his master most, the Pharisee answered correctly, "The one, to whom the master forgave most." And Jesus does not fail to make him observe: "Thou hast judged rightly (Lk 7:43)." Only when the judgment of Simon is turned toward love: then is he in the right.

24 HOURS FOR THE LORD, ST. PETER'S BASILICA
FRIDAY, MARCH 13, 2015

Do Not Judge Others

The Lord Jesus shows us the steps of the pilgrimage to attain our goal: "Judge not, and you will not be judged; condemn not, and you will not be condemned; forgive, and you will be forgiven; give, and it will be given to you; good measure, pressed down, shaken together, running over, will be put into your lap. For the measure you give will be the measure you get back" (Lk 6:37–38). The Lord asks us above all not to judge and not to condemn. If anyone wishes to avoid God's judgment, he should not make himself the judge of his brother or sister. Human beings, whenever they judge, look no farther than the surface, whereas the Father looks into the very depths of the soul. How much harm words do when they are motivated by feelings of jealousy and envy! To speak ill of others puts them in a bad light, undermines their reputation and leaves them prey to the whims of gossip. To refrain from judgment and condemnation means, in a positive sense, to know how to accept the good in every person and to spare him any suffering that might be caused by our partial judgment, our presumption to know everything about him. But this is still not sufficient to express mercy. Jesus asks us also to forgive and to give. To be instruments of mercy because it was we who first received mercy from God. To be generous with others, knowing that God showers his goodness upon us with immense generosity.

MISERICORDIAE VULTUS, BULL OF INDICTION OF THE EXTRAORDINARY JUBILEE YEAR OF MERCY, 14

GOD KNOWS HOW TO WAIT

At times we are in a great hurry to judge, to categorize, to put the good here, the bad there.... But remember the prayer of that self-righteous man: "God, I thank you that I am good, that I am not like other men, malicious" (cf. Lk 18:11–12). God, however, knows how to wait. With patience and mercy he gazes into the "field" of life of every person; he sees much better than we do the filth and the evil, but he also sees the seeds of good and waits with trust for them to grow. God is patient, he knows how to wait. This is so beautiful: our God is a patient father, who always waits for us and waits with his heart in hand to welcome us, to forgive us. He always forgives us if we go to him.

ANGELUS, ST. PETER'S SQUARE
SUNDAY, JULY 20, 2014

We Will Be Judged by the Measure We Use

In the end, in fact, evil will be removed and eliminated: at the time of harvest, that is, of judgment, the harvesters will follow the orders of the field owner, separating the weed to burn it (cf. Mt 13:30). On the day of the final harvest, the judge will be Jesus, He who has sown good grain in the world and who himself became the "grain of wheat," who died and rose. In the end we will all be judged by the same measure with which we have judged: the mercy we have shown to others will also be shown to us. Let us ask Our Lady, our Mother, to help us to grow in patience, in hope and in mercy with all brothers and sisters.

ANGELUS, ST. PETER'S SQUARE
SUNDAY, JULY 20, 2014

An Attitude of Repentance

In the presence of a repentant people, God's justice is transformed into mercy and forgiveness. This challenges us by inviting us to make room for this same inner attitude. To become merciful, we must first acknowledge that we have done many things wrong: we are sinners! We need to know how to say: "Lord, I am ashamed of what I have done in life." If we act in this way, how many good things will follow. With this attitude of repentance we will be more capable of being merciful, because we will feel God's mercy for us. In the Our Father, in fact, we do not only pray: "forgive us our trespasses." We also pray "forgive us as we forgive those who trespass against us."

MORNING MEDITATION IN THE CHAPEL OF THE
DOMUS SANCTAE MARTHAE
MONDAY, MARCH 17, 2014

What Does it Mean to Open One's Heart?

We need an openness to expanding our hearts. It is precisely shame and repentance that expands a small, selfish heart, since they give space to God to forgive us. What does it mean to open and expand one's heart? First, it means acknowledging ourselves to be sinners and not looking to what others have done. And from here, the basic question becomes: "Who am I to judge this? Who am I to gossip about this? Who am I, who have done the same things, or worse?" You can receive far more if you have a big heart! A big heart doesn't get entangled in other people's lives, it doesn't condemn but forgives and forgets as God has forgiven and forgotten my sins.

MORNING MEDITATION IN THE CHAPEL OF THE
DOMUS SANCTAE MARTHAE
MONDAY, MARCH 17, 2014

MERCY COMES THROUGH KNOWING OUR OWN FAULTS
In order to be merciful we need to call upon the Lord's help, since it is a grace. And we also need to recognize our sins and be ashamed of them and forgive and forget the offenses of others. Men and women who are merciful have big, big hearts: they always excuse others and think more of their own sins. Were someone to say to them: "But do you see what so and so did?", they respond in mercy saying: "But I have enough to be concerned over with all I have done."

MORNING MEDITATION IN THE CHAPEL OF THE
DOMUS SANCTAE MARTHAE
MONDAY, MARCH 17, 2014

Justice and Mercy

It would not be out of place at this point to recall the relationship between justice and mercy. These are not two contradictory realities, but two dimensions of a single reality that unfolds progressively until it culminates in the fullness of love. Justice is a fundamental concept for civil society, which is meant to be governed by the rule of law. Justice is also understood as that which is rightly due to each individual. In the Bible, there are many references to divine justice and to God as "judge." In these passages, justice is understood as the full observance of the Law and the behavior of every good Israelite in conformity with God's commandments. Such a vision, however, has not infrequently led to legalism by distorting the original meaning of justice and obscuring its profound value. To overcome this legalistic perspective, we need to recall that in Sacred Scripture, justice is conceived essentially as the faithful abandonment of oneself to God's will.

MISERICORDIAE VULTUS, BULL OF INDICTION OF THE
EXTRAORDINARY JUBILEE YEAR OF MERCY, 20

God Desires Mercy, Not Sacrifice

For his part, Jesus speaks several times of the importance of faith over and above the observance of the law. It is in this sense that we must understand his words when, reclining at table with Matthew and other tax collectors and sinners, he says to the Pharisees raising objections to him, "Go and learn the meaning of 'I desire mercy not sacrifice.' I have come not to call the righteous, but sinners" (Mt 9:13). Faced with a vision of justice as the mere observance of the law that judges people simply by dividing them into two groups—the just and sinners—Jesus is bent on revealing the great gift of mercy that searches out sinners and offers them pardon and salvation.

MISERICORDIAE VULTUS, BULL OF INDICTION OF THE
EXTRAORDINARY JUBILEE YEAR OF MERCY, 20

Mercy Is the Very Nature of God

If God limited himself to only justice, he would cease to be God, and would instead be like human beings who ask merely that the law be respected. But mere justice is not enough. Experience shows that an appeal to justice alone will result in its destruction. This is why God goes beyond justice with his mercy and forgiveness. Yet this does not mean that justice should be devalued or rendered superfluous. On the contrary: anyone who makes a mistake must pay the price. However, this is just the beginning of conversion, not its end, because one begins to feel the tenderness and mercy of God. God does not deny justice. He rather envelops it and surpasses it with an even greater event in which we experience love as the foundation of true justice.

MISERICORDIAE VULTUS, BULL OF INDICTION OF THE EXTRAORDINARY JUBILEE YEAR OF MERCY, 21

LOVING OUR ENEMIES

Jesus gave us the law of love: to love God and to love one another as brothers. And the Lord did not fail to explain it a bit further, with the Beatitudes, which nicely summarize the Christian approach. Let us look first of all at the verbs Jesus uses: love; do good; bless; pray; offer; do not refuse; give. With these words, Jesus shows us the path that we must take, a path of generosity. He asks us first and foremost to love. And we ask, "Whom must I love?" He answers us, "Your enemies." And, with surprise, we ask for confirmation: "Our actual enemies?" "Yes," the Lord tells us, actually "your enemies!" But the Lord also asks us to "do good." And if we do not ask him, "to whom?" he tells us straight away, "to those who hate us." And this time too, we ask the Lord for confirmation: "But must I do good to those who hate me?" And the Lord's reply is again, "yes." Then he even asks us to "bless those who curse us." And to "pray" not only "for my mama, for my dad, my children, my family," but "for those who abuse us." And "not to refuse anyone who begs from you."

MORNING MEDITATION IN THE CHAPEL OF THE
DOMUS SANCTAE MARTHAE
THURSDAY, SEPTEMBER 11, 2014

What Makes the Gospel New?

The newness of the Gospel lies in the giving of oneself, giving the heart, to those who actually dislike us, who harm us, to our enemies. The Gospel is a new message that is difficult to carry forward. In a word, it means go behind Jesus. Follow him. Imitate him. Jesus does not answer his Father by saying, "I shall go and say a few words, I shall make a nice speech, I shall point the way and then come back." No, Jesus' response to the Father is: "I shall do your will." And indeed, in the Mount of Olives he says to the Father: "Thy will be done." And thus "he gives his life, not for his friends" but "for his enemies!"

MORNING MEDITATION IN THE CHAPEL OF THE
DOMUS SANCTAE MARTHAE
THURSDAY, SEPTEMBER 11, 2014

The Christian Way

The Christian way is not easy, but this is it. To those who say, "I don't feel like doing this," the response is "if you don't feel like it, that's your problem, but this is the Christian way. This is the path that Jesus teaches us. The reason to take the path of Jesus, which is mercy, is that only with a merciful heart can we do all that the Lord advises us, until the end. The Christian life is not a self-reflexive life but it comes outside of itself to give to others: it is a gift, it is love, and love does not turn back on itself, it is not selfish: it gives itself!

MORNING MEDITATION IN THE CHAPEL OF THE
DOMUS SANCTAE MARTHAE
THURSDAY, SEPTEMBER 11, 2014

"As We Forgive"

The passage of St. Luke concludes with the invitation not to judge and to be merciful. It often seems that we have been appointed judges of others: gossiping, criticizing, we judge everyone. But Jesus tells us: "Judge not and you will not be judged; condemn not, and you will not be condemned; forgive, and you will be forgiven." And so, we say it every day in the Our Father: "forgive us as we forgive." If I do not first forgive, how can I ask the Father to forgive me? There is also another really beautiful image in the Gospel reading: "Give and it will be given to you." Jesus' heart can be seen to grow and he makes this promise which is perhaps an image of heaven.

MORNING MEDITATION IN THE CHAPEL OF THE
DOMUS SANCTAE MARTHAE
THURSDAY, SEPTEMBER 11, 2014

Being Christian Isn't Easy

A first reading of Chapter Six of Luke's Gospel is unnerving. But, if we take the Gospel and we give it a second, a third, a fourth reading, we can then ask the Lord for the grace to understand what it is to be Christian. Being Christian isn't easy and we cannot become Christian with our own strength; we need the grace of God. There is a prayer which should be said every day: "Lord, grant me the grace to become a good Christian, because I cannot do it alone."

MORNING MEDITATION IN THE CHAPEL OF THE
DOMUS SANCTAE MARTHAE
THURSDAY, SEPTEMBER 11, 2014

CHAPTER FIVE

~ The Cross: No Greater Love ~

Through the Cross We Receive New Life

God's justice is his mercy given to everyone as a grace that flows from the death and resurrection of Jesus Christ. Thus the Cross of Christ is God's judgment on all of us and on the whole world, because through it he offers us the certitude of love and new life.

MISERICORDIAE VULTUS, BULL OF INDICTION OF THE EXTRAORDINARY JUBILEE YEAR OF MERCY, 21

THE IMMEASURABLE GIFT OF REDEMPTION

Lent comes to us as a providential time to change course, to recover the ability to react to the reality of evil which always challenges us. Lent is to be lived as a time of conversion, as a time of renewal for individuals and communities, by drawing close to God and by trustfully adhering to the Gospel. In this way, it also allows us to look with new eyes at our brothers and sisters and their needs. That is why Lent is a favorable time to convert to the love of God and neighbor; a love that knows how to make its own the Lord's attitude of gratuitousness and mercy— who "became poor, so that by his poverty you might become rich" (cf. 2 Cor 8:9). In meditating on the central mysteries of the Faith, the Passion, Cross and Resurrection of Christ, we shall realize that the immeasurable gift of the Redemption has been granted to us through God's free initiative.

GENERAL AUDIENCE, ST. PETER'S SQUARE
ASH WEDNESDAY, MARCH 5, 2014

The Immensity of God's Mercy

God placed on Jesus' Cross all the weight of our sins, all the injustices perpetrated by every Cain against his brother, all the bitterness of the betrayal by Judas and by Peter, all the vanity of tyrants, all the arrogance of false friends. It was a heavy Cross, like night experienced by abandoned people, heavy like the death of loved ones, heavy because it carries all the ugliness of evil. However, the Cross is also glorious like the dawn after a long night, for it represents all the love of God, which is greater than our iniquities and our betrayals. In the Cross we see the monstrosity of man, when he allows evil to guide him; but we also see the immensity of the mercy of God, who does not treat us according to our sins but according to his mercy.

WAY OF THE CROSS AT THE COLOSSEUM, PALATINE HILL
GOOD FRIDAY, APRIL 18, 2014

Finding Hope in the Cross

Before the Cross of Jesus, we apprehend in a way that we can almost touch with our hands how much we are eternally loved; before the Cross we feel that we are "children" and not "things" or "objects." Finally, all together, let us remember the sick, let us remember all those who have been abandoned under the weight of the Cross, that they may find in the trial of the Cross the strength of hope, of hope, in the resurrection and love of God.

WAY OF THE CROSS AT THE COLOSSEUM, PALATINE HILL
GOOD FRIDAY, APRIL 18, 2014

A Sign of Love

When we look to the Cross where Jesus was nailed, we contemplate the sign of love, of the infinite love of God for each of us and the source of our salvation. The mercy of God, which embraces the whole world, springs from the Cross. Through the Cross of Christ the Evil One is overcome, death is defeated, life is given to us, hope is restored. This is important: through the Cross of Christ hope is restored to us. The Cross of Jesus is our one true hope! That is why the Church "exalts" the Holy Cross, and why we Christians bless ourselves with the sign of the cross. That is, we don't exalt crosses, but the glorious Cross of Christ, the sign of God's immense love, the sign of our salvation and path toward the Resurrection. This is our hope.

ANGELUS, ST. PETER'S SQUARE
SUNDAY, SEPTEMBER 14, 2014

THE STUPENDOUS MYSTERY OF GOD'S LOVE

Awareness of the marvels that the Lord has wrought for our salvation disposes our minds and hearts to an attitude of thanksgiving to God for all that he has given us, for all that he has accomplished for the good of his People and for the whole of humanity. This marks the beginning of our conversion: it is the grateful response to the stupendous mystery of God's love. When we see the love that God has for us, we feel the desire to draw close to him: this is conversion.

GENERAL AUDIENCE, ST. PETER'S SQUARE
ASH WEDNESDAY, MARCH 5, 2014

Purified and Renewed in the Spirit

Let us give thanks to God for the mystery of his crucified love; authentic faith, conversion and openness of heart to the brethren: these are the essential elements for living the season of Lent. On this journey, we want to invoke with special trust the protection and help of the Virgin Mary: may she, who was the first to believe in Christ, accompany us in our days of intense prayer and penance, so that we might come to celebrate, purified and renewed in spirit, the great Paschal mystery of her Son.

GENERAL AUDIENCE, ST. PETER'S SQUARE
ASH WEDNESDAY, MARCH 5, 2014

CHRIST'S GREAT WORK OF MERCY

Jesus insists on the conditions for being his disciples: preferring nothing to the love of Christ, carrying one's cross and following him. Many people in fact drew near to Jesus, they wanted to be included among his followers; and this would happen especially after some miraculous sign which accredited him as the Messiah, the King of Israel. However Jesus did not want to disappoint anyone. He knew well what awaited him in Jerusalem and which path the Father was asking him to take: it was the Way of the Cross, the way of sacrificing himself for the forgiveness of our sins. Following Jesus does not mean taking part in a triumphal procession! It means sharing his merciful love, entering his great work of mercy for each and every man and for all men.

ANGELUS, ST. PETER'S SQUARE
SUNDAY, SEPTEMBER 8, 2013

FOOLISH CHRISTIANS

The Christian life, as Jesus presents it, seems truly to be folly. St. Paul himself speaks of "the folly of the cross of Christ, which is not part of the wisdom of the world." To be a Christian is to become a bit foolish, in a certain sense, and to renounce that worldly shrewdness in order to do all that Jesus tells us to do. And, if we make an accounting, if we balance things out, it seems to weigh against us. But the path of Jesus is magnanimity, generosity, the giving of oneself without measure. He came into the world to save and he gave himself, he forgave, he spoke ill of no one, he did not judge.

MORNING MEDITATION IN THE CHAPEL OF THE
DOMUS SANCTAE MARTHAE
THURSDAY, SEPTEMBER 11, 2014

HUMAN JUSTICE AND DIVINE JUSTICE

If we live according to the law "an eye for an eye, a tooth for a tooth," we will never escape from the spiral of evil. The evil one is clever, and deludes us into thinking that with our human justice we can save ourselves and save the world! In reality, only the justice of God can save us! And the justice of God is revealed in the Cross: the Cross is the judgment of God on us all and on this world. But how does God judge us? By giving his life for us! Here is the supreme act of justice that defeated the prince of this world once and for all; and this supreme act of justice is the supreme act of mercy. Jesus calls us all to follow this path: "Be merciful, even as your Father is merciful" (Lk 6:36). I now ask of you one thing. In silence, let's all think... everyone think of a person with whom we are annoyed, with whom we are angry, someone we do not like. Let us think of that person and in silence, at this moment, let us pray for this person and let us become merciful with this person.

ANGELUS, ST. PETER'S SQUARE
SUNDAY, SEPTEMBER 15, 2013

Jesus Is the Path

Looking at Jesus we see he chose the path of humility and service. Rather, he himself is this path. Jesus was not indecisive; he was not indifferent. He made a decision and followed it through until the end. He decided to become man and as a man to become a servant until his death on the Cross. This is the way of love, there is no other. Therefore we see that love is not simply social assistance and not in the least social assistance to reassure consciences. No, that is not love, that is business, those are transactions. Love is free. Charity, love is…a way of being, a way of life, it is a path of humility and of solidarity. There is no other way for this love: to be humble and in solidarity with others.

MEETING WITH THE POOR AND PRISON INMATES,
CATHEDRAL OF CAGLIARI
SUNDAY, SEPTEMBER 22, 2013

CHAPTER SIX

~ Mercy and Resurrection: Our Eternal Hope ~

Love Has Triumphed

What a joy it is for me to announce this message: Christ is risen! I would like it to go out to every house and every family, especially where the suffering is greatest, in hospitals, in prisons…

Most of all, I would like it to enter every heart, for it is there that God wants to sow this Good News: Jesus is risen, there is hope for you, you are no longer in the power of sin, of evil! Love has triumphed, mercy has been victorious! The mercy of God always triumphs!

URBI ET ORBI MESSAGE
EASTER SUNDAY, MARCH 31, 2013

LET US ACCEPT THE GRACE OF CHRIST'S RESURRECTION! Let us be renewed by God's mercy, let us be loved by Jesus, let us enable the power of his love to transform our lives too; and let us become agents of this mercy, channels through which God can water the earth, protect all creation and make justice and peace flourish. And so we ask the risen Jesus, who turns death into life, to change hatred into love, vengeance into forgiveness, war into peace. Yes, Christ is our peace, and through him we implore peace for all the world.

URBI ET ORBI MESSAGE
EASTER SUNDAY, MARCH 31, 2013

We Are Searching to Meet Jesus

In the redeeming contact with the wounds of the Risen One, Thomas showed his own wounds, his own injuries, his own lacerations, his own humiliation; in the print of the nails he found the decisive proof that he was loved, that he was expected, that he was understood. He found himself before the Messiah filled with kindness, mercy, tenderness. This was the Lord he was searching for, he, in the hidden depths of his being, for he had always known He was like this. And how many of us are searching deep in our heart to meet Jesus, just as He is: kind, merciful, tender! For we know, deep down, that He is like this.

REGINA CÆLI, ST. PETER'S SQUARE
SECOND SUNDAY OF EASTER—DIVINE MERCY SUNDAY
APRIL 12, 2015

Touching the Paschal Mystery

Having rediscovered personal contact with Christ who is amiable and mercifully patient, Thomas understood the profound significance of his Resurrection and, intimately transformed, he declared his full and total faith in Him exclaiming: "My Lord and my God!" [John 20:28]. Beautiful, Thomas' expression is beautiful! He was able to "touch" the Paschal Mystery which fully demonstrated God's redeeming love (cf. Eph 2:4). All of us too are like Thomas: we are called to contemplate, in the wounds of the Risen One, Divine Mercy, which overcomes all human limitations and shines on the darkness of evil and of sin.

REGINA CÆLI, ST. PETER'S SQUARE
SECOND SUNDAY OF EASTER—DIVINE MERCY SUNDAY
APRIL 12, 2015

DIVINE MERCY, UNFAILING LOVE

The Second Sunday of Easter [is] also known as "Divine Mercy Sunday." What a beautiful truth of faith this is for our lives: the mercy of God! God's love for us is so great, so deep; it is an unfailing love, one which always takes us by the hand and supports us, lifts us up and leads us on.

BASILICA OF ST. JOHN LATERAN
SECOND SUNDAY OF EASTER—DIVINE MERCY SUNDAY
APRIL 7, 2013

The Face of the Risen Jesus

The Apostle Thomas personally experiences this mercy of God, which has a concrete face, the face of Jesus, the risen Jesus. Thomas does not believe it when the other Apostles tell him: "We have seen the Lord." It isn't enough for him that Jesus had foretold it, promised it: "On the third day I will rise." He wants to see, he wants to put his hand in the place of the nails and in Jesus' side. And how does Jesus react? With patience: Jesus does not abandon Thomas in his stubborn unbelief; he gives him a week's time, he does not close the door, he waits. And Thomas acknowledges his own poverty, his little faith. "My Lord and my God!": with this simple yet faith-filled invocation, he responds to Jesus' patience. He lets himself be enveloped by divine mercy; he sees it before his eyes, in the wounds of Christ's hands and feet and in his open side, and he discovers trust: he is a new man, no longer an unbeliever, but a believer.

BASILICA OF ST. JOHN LATERAN
SECOND SUNDAY OF EASTER—DIVINE MERCY SUNDAY
APRIL 7, 2013

Finding Mercy in Weakness

Let us also remember Peter: three times he denied Jesus, precisely when he should have been closest to him; and when he hits bottom he meets the gaze of Jesus who patiently, wordlessly, says to him: "Peter, don't be afraid of your weakness, trust in me." Peter understands, he feels the loving gaze of Jesus, and he weeps. How beautiful is this gaze of Jesus—how much tenderness is there! Brothers and sisters, let us never lose trust in the patience and mercy of God!

BASILICA OF ST. JOHN LATERAN
SECOND SUNDAY OF EASTER—DIVINE MERCY SUNDAY
APRIL 7, 2013

FINDING MERCY IN OUR MOMENTS OF DESPAIR

Let us think too of the two disciples on the way to Emmaus: their sad faces, their barren journey, their despair. But Jesus does not abandon them: he walks beside them, and not only that! Patiently he explains the Scriptures which spoke of him, and he stays to share a meal with them. This is God's way of doing things: he is not impatient like us, who often want everything all at once, even in our dealings with other people. God is patient with us because he loves us, and those who love are able to understand, to hope, to inspire confidence; they do not give up, they do not burn bridges, they are able to forgive. Let us remember this in our lives as Christians: God always waits for us, even when we have left him behind! He is never far from us, and if we return to him, he is ready to embrace us.

BASILICA OF ST. JOHN LATERAN
SECOND SUNDAY OF EASTER—DIVINE MERCY SUNDAY
APRIL 7, 2013

Letting Ourselves Be Loved

Dear brothers and sisters, let us be enveloped by the mercy of God; let us trust in his patience, which always gives us more time. Let us find the courage to return to his house, to dwell in his loving wounds, allowing ourselves be loved by him and to encounter his mercy in the sacraments. We will feel his wonderful tenderness, we will feel his embrace, and we too will become more capable of mercy, patience, forgiveness and love.

BASILICA OF ST. JOHN LATERAN
SECOND SUNDAY OF EASTER—DIVINE MERCY SUNDAY
APRIL 7, 2013

The Beatitude of Faith

Jesus said: "Have you believed because you have seen me? Blessed are those who have not seen and yet believe" [John 20:29]; and who were those who believed without seeing? Other disciples, other men and women of Jerusalem, who, on the testimony of the Apostles and the women, believed, even though they had not met the Risen Jesus. This is a very important word about faith, we can call it the beatitude of faith. Blessed are those who have not seen but have believed: this is the beatitude of faith! In every epoch and in every place blessed are those who, on the strength of the word of God proclaimed in the Church and witnessed by Christians, believe that Jesus Christ is the love of God incarnate, Mercy incarnate. And this applies for each one of us!

REGINA CÆLI, ST. PETER'S SQUARE
SECOND SUNDAY OF EASTER—DIVINE MERCY SUNDAY
APRIL 7, 2013

A Torrent of Mercy

Let us receive the special grace of this moment. We pause in reverent silence before this empty tomb in order to rediscover the grandeur of our Christian vocation: we are men and women of resurrection, and not of death. From this place we learn how to live our lives, the trials of our Churches and of the whole world, in the light of Easter morning. Every injury, every one of our pains and sorrows, has been borne on the shoulders of the Good Shepherd who offered himself in sacrifice and thereby opened the way to eternal life. His open wounds are like the cleft through which the torrent of his mercy is poured out upon the world. Let us not allow ourselves to be robbed of the basis of our hope, which is this: *Christòs anesti!* Let us not deprive the world of the joyful message of the resurrection! And let us not be deaf to the powerful summons to unity which rings out from this very place, in the words of the One who, risen from the dead, calls all of us "my brothers" (cf. Mt 28:10; Jn 20:17).

BASILICA OF THE HOLY SEPULCHRE (JERUSALEM)
SUNDAY, MAY 25, 2014

CHAPTER SEVEN

~ Mary: Mother of Mercy ~

A LIFE PATTERNED AFTER MERCY

My thoughts now turn to the Mother of Mercy. May the sweetness of her countenance watch over us in this Holy Year, so that all of us may rediscover the joy of God's tenderness. No one has penetrated the profound mystery of the incarnation like Mary. Her entire life was patterned after the presence of mercy made flesh. The Mother of the Crucified and Risen One has entered the sanctuary of divine mercy because she participated intimately in the mystery of His love.

MISERICORDIAE VULTUS, BULL OF INDICTION OF THE
EXTRAORDINARY JUBILEE YEAR OF MERCY, 24

SHE TREASURED DIVINE MERCY IN HER HEART

Chosen to be the Mother of the Son of God, Mary, from the outset, was prepared by the love of God to be the Ark of the Covenant between God and man. She treasured divine mercy in her heart in perfect harmony with her Son Jesus. Her hymn of praise, sung at the threshold of the home of Elizabeth, was dedicated to the mercy of God which extends from "generation to generation" (Lk 1:50). We too were included in those prophetic words of the Virgin Mary. This will be a source of comfort and strength to us as we cross the threshold of the Holy Year to experience the fruits of divine mercy.

MISERICORDIAE VULTUS, BULL OF INDICTION OF THE EXTRAORDINARY JUBILEE YEAR OF MERCY, 24

THE FULLNESS OF MERCY

The Solemnity of the Immaculate Conception recalls God's action from the very beginning of the history of mankind. After the sin of Adam and Eve, God did not wish to leave humanity alone in the throes of evil. And so he turned his gaze to Mary, holy and immaculate in love (cf. Eph 1:4), choosing her to be the Mother of man's Redeemer. When faced with the gravity of sin, God responds with the fullness of mercy. Mercy will always be greater than any sin, and no one can place limits on the love of God who is ever ready to forgive.

MISERICORDIAE VULTUS, BULL OF INDICTION OF THE EXTRAORDINARY JUBILEE YEAR OF MERCY, 3

MARY, OUR GUIDE

May our beloved Mother, Mary Most Holy, go with us and sustain us all. May she teach us to take the path of joy, to experience this joy! That was the high point—this joy, this meeting of Jesus and Mary, and we can imagine what it was like. Their meeting was the high point of Mary's journey of faith, and that of the whole Church. What is our faith like? Like Mary, do we keep it burning even at times of difficulty, in moments of darkness? Do I feel the joy of faith?

ANGELUS, ST. PETER'S SQUARE
SATURDAY, JUNE 29, 2013

Making Fruitful God's Mercy

I am convinced that the whole Church will find in this Jubilee the joy needed to rediscover and make fruitful the mercy of God, with which all of us are called to give consolation to every man and woman of our time. From this moment, we entrust this Holy Year to the Mother of Mercy, that she might turn her gaze upon us and watch over our journey.

24 HOURS FOR THE LORD, ST. PETER'S BASILICA
FRIDAY, MARCH 13, 2015

Mary, the Undoer of Knots

We know one thing: nothing is impossible for God's mercy! Even the most tangled knots are loosened by his grace. And Mary, whose "yes" opened the door for God to undo the knot of the ancient disobedience, is the Mother who patiently and lovingly brings us to God, so that he can untangle the knots of our soul by his fatherly mercy. We all have some of these knots and we can ask in our heart of hearts: What are the knots in my life? "Father, my knots cannot be undone!" It is a mistake to say anything of the sort! All the knots of our heart, every knot of our conscience, can be undone. Do I ask Mary to help me trust in God's mercy, to undo those knots, to change? She, as a woman of faith, will surely tell you: "Get up, go to the Lord: he understands you." And she leads us by the hand as a Mother, our Mother, to the embrace of our Father, the Father of mercies.

PRAYER FOR THE MARIAN DAY, ST. PETER'S SQUARE
SATURDAY, OCTOBER 12, 2013

GIVING JESUS OUR FLESH

Do we think that Jesus' incarnation is simply a past event which has nothing to do with us personally? Believing in Jesus means giving him our flesh with the humility and courage of Mary, so that he can continue to dwell in our midst. It means giving him our hands, to caress the little ones and the poor; our feet, to go forth and meet our brothers and sisters; our arms, to hold up the weak and to work in the Lord's vineyard, our minds, to think and act in the light of the Gospel; and especially to offer our hearts to love and to make choices in accordance with God's will. All this happens thanks to the working of the Holy Spirit. And in this way we become instruments in God's hands, so that Jesus can act in the world through us.

PRAYER FOR THE MARIAN DAY, ST. PETER'S SQUARE
SATURDAY, OCTOBER 12, 2013

Mercy Knows No Bounds

At the foot of the Cross, Mary, together with John, the disciple of love, witnessed the words of forgiveness spoken by Jesus. This supreme expression of mercy towards those who crucified him show us the point to which the mercy of God can reach. Mary attests that the mercy of the Son of God knows no bounds and extends to everyone, without exception. Let us address her in the words of the Salve Regina, a prayer ever ancient and ever new, so that she may never tire of turning her merciful eyes upon us, and make us worthy to contemplate the face of mercy, her Son Jesus.

MISERICORDIAE VULTUS, BULL OF INDICTION OF THE
EXTRAORDINARY JUBILEE YEAR OF MERCY, 24

Mary's Immense Trust

The Lord does not give the same things to everyone in the same way: He knows us personally and entrusts us with what is right for us; but in everyone, in all, there is something equal: the same, immense trust. God trusts us, God has hope in us! And this is the same for everyone. Let us not disappoint Him! Let us not be misled by fear, but let us reciprocate trust with trust! The Virgin Mary embodied this attitude in the fullest and most beautiful way. She received and welcomed the most sublime gift, Jesus himself, and in turn she offered Him to mankind with a generous heart. Let us ask her to help us to be "good and faithful servants" in order to participate "in the joy of our Lord."

ANGELUS, ST. PETER'S SQUARE
SUNDAY, NOVEMBER 16, 2014

A MOTHER'S MERCY FOR HER CHILDREN

The mercy of Jesus is not only an emotion; it is a force which gives life that raises man! Today's Gospel also tells us this in the episode of the widow of Nain (Lk 7:11–17). With his disciples, Jesus arrives in Nain, a village in Galilee, right at the moment when a funeral is taking place. A boy, the only son of a widow, is being carried for burial. Jesus immediately fixes his gaze on the crying mother. The Evangelist Luke says: "And when the Lord saw her, he had compassion on her" (v. 13). This "compassion" is God's love for man, it is mercy, thus the attitude of God in contact with human misery, with our destitution, our suffering, our anguish. The biblical term "compassion" recalls a mother's womb. The mother in fact reacts in a way all her own in confronting the pain of her children. It is in this way, according to Scripture, that God loves us.

ANGELUS, ST. PETER'S SQUARE
SUNDAY, JUNE 9, 2013, FEAST OF THE SACRED HEART

God's Mercy Gives Life

What is the fruit of this love and mercy? It is life! Jesus says to the widow of Nain: "Do not weep" and then he calls the dead boy and awakes him as if from sleep (cf. vv. 13–15). Let's think about this, it's beautiful: God's mercy gives life to man, it raises him from the dead. Let us not forget that the Lord always watches over us with mercy; he always watches over us with mercy. Let us not be afraid of approaching him! He has a merciful heart! If we show him our inner wounds, our inner sins, he will always forgive us. It is pure mercy. Let us go to Jesus!

ANGELUS, ST. PETER'S SQUARE
SUNDAY, JUNE 9, 2013, FEAST OF THE SACRED HEART

Mary's Immaculate Heart

Let us turn to the Virgin Mary: her Immaculate Heart, a mother's heart, has fully shared in the "compassion" of God, especially in the hour of the passion and death of Jesus. May Mary help us to be mild, humble and merciful with our brothers.

ANGELUS, ST. PETER'S SQUARE
SUNDAY, JUNE 9, 2013, FEAST OF THE SACRED HEART

CHAPTER EIGHT

~ The Church: The Place Where We Meet Mercy ~

THE GREAT RIVER OF MERCY

In this Jubilee Year, let us allow God to surprise us. He never tires of casting open the doors of his heart and of repeating that he loves us and wants to share his love with us. The Church feels the urgent need to proclaim God's mercy. Her life is authentic and credible only when she becomes a convincing herald of mercy. She knows that her primary task, especially at a moment full of great hopes and signs of contradiction, is to introduce everyone to the great mystery of God's mercy by contemplating the face of Christ. The Church is called above all to be a credible witness to mercy, professing it and living it as the core of the revelation of Jesus Christ. From the heart of the Trinity, from the depths of the mystery of God, the great river of mercy wells up and overflows unceasingly. It is a spring that will never run dry, no matter how many people draw from it. Every time someone is in need, he or she can approach it, because the mercy of God never ends. The profundity of the mystery surrounding it is as inexhaustible as the richness which springs up from it.

MISERICORDIAE VULTUS, BULL OF INDICTION OF THE EXTRAORDINARY JUBILEE YEAR OF MERCY, 25

Mindful of God's Mercy

In this Jubilee Year, may the Church echo the word of God that resounds strong and clear as a message and a sign of pardon, strength, aid, and love. May she never tire of extending mercy, and be ever patient in offering compassion and comfort. May the Church become the voice of every man and woman, and repeat confidently without end: "Be mindful of your mercy, O Lord, and your steadfast love, for they have been from of old" (Ps 25:6).

MISERICORDIAE VULTUS, BULL OF INDICTION OF THE
EXTRAORDINARY JUBILEE YEAR OF MERCY, 25

Servant of Christ's Love

The Church's first truth is the love of Christ. The Church makes herself a servant of this love and mediates it to all people: a love that forgives and expresses itself in the gift of oneself. Consequently, wherever the Church is present, the mercy of the Father must be evident. In our parishes, communities, associations and movements, in a word, wherever there are Christians, everyone should find an oasis of mercy.

MISERICORDIAE VULTUS, BULL OF INDICTION OF THE
EXTRAORDINARY JUBILEE YEAR OF MERCY, 12

An Endless Desire to Show Mercy

Mercy is the very foundation of the Church's life. All of her pastoral activity should be caught up in the tenderness she makes present to believers; nothing in her preaching and in her witness to the world can be lacking in mercy. The Church's very credibility is seen in how she shows merciful and compassionate love. The Church "has an endless desire to show mercy" [*Evangelii Gaudium*, 24].

MISERICORDIAE VULTUS, BULL OF INDICTION OF THE EXTRAORDINARY JUBILEE YEAR OF MERCY, 10

Strive for a Higher Goal

Perhaps we have long since forgotten how to show and live the way of mercy. The temptation, on the one hand, to focus exclusively on justice made us forget that this is only the first, albeit necessary and indispensable step. But the Church needs to go beyond and strive for a higher and more important goal. On the other hand, sad to say, we must admit that the practice of mercy is waning in the wider culture. In some cases the word seems to have dropped out of use. However, without a witness to mercy, life becomes fruitless and sterile, as if sequestered in a barren desert.

MISERICORDIAE VULTUS, BULL OF INDICTION OF THE EXTRAORDINARY JUBILEE YEAR OF MERCY, 10

The Joyful Call to Mercy

The time has come for the Church to take up the joyful call to mercy once more. It is time to return to the basics and to bear the weaknesses and struggles of our brothers and sisters. Mercy is the force that reawakens us to new life and instills in us the courage to look to the future with hope.

MISERICORDIAE VULTUS, BULL OF INDICTION OF THE EXTRAORDINARY JUBILEE YEAR OF MERCY, 10

God Is Always First

The love of God precedes everything. God is always first, He arrives before us, He precedes us. ... When we arrive He is waiting for us, He calls us, He makes us walk. Always anticipating us. And this is called love, because God always waits for us. "But, Father, I don't believe this, because if you only knew, Father; my life was so horrible, how can I think that God is waiting for me?" "God is waiting for you. And if you were a great sinner He is waiting for you even more and waiting for you with great love, because He is first. This is the beauty of the Church, who leads us to this God who is waiting for us!

GENERAL AUDIENCE, ST. PETER'S SQUARE
WEDNESDAY, JUNE 18, 2014

GOD EXCLUDES NO ONE

No one is excluded from life's hope, from God's love. The Church is sent to reawaken this hope everywhere, especially where it has been suffocated by difficult and oftentimes inhuman living conditions; where hope cannot breathe it suffocates. We need the fresh air of the Gospel, the breath of the Spirit of the Risen Christ, to rekindle it in people's hearts. The Church is the home where the doors are always open, not only because everyone finds a welcome and is able to breathe in love and hope, but also because we can go out bearing this love and this hope. The Holy Spirit urges us to go beyond our own narrow confines and he guides us to the outskirts of humanity.

ADDRESS TO PARTICIPANTS IN THE PLENARY OF THE
PONTIFICAL COUNCIL FOR PROMOTING THE NEW
EVANGELIZATION, CLEMENTINE HALL
MONDAY, OCTOBER 14, 2013

GOD'S MERCIFUL INDULGENCE

The Church lives within the communion of the saints. In the Eucharist, this communion, which is a gift from God, becomes a spiritual union binding us to the saints and blessed ones whose number is beyond counting (cf. Rev 7:4). Their holiness comes to the aid of our weakness in a way that enables the Church, with her maternal prayers and her way of life, to fortify the weakness of some with the strength of others. Hence, to live the indulgence of the Holy Year means to approach the Father's mercy with the certainty that his forgiveness extends to the entire life of the believer. To gain an indulgence is to experience the holiness of the Church, who bestows upon all the fruits of Christ's redemption, so that God's love and forgiveness may extend everywhere. Let us live this Jubilee intensely, begging the Father to forgive our sins and to bathe us in his merciful "indulgence."

MISERICORDIAE VULTUS, BULL OF INDICTION OF THE EXTRAORDINARY JUBILEE YEAR OF MERCY, 22

THE CHURCH BRINGS US TO GOD

Still today some say: "Christ yes, the Church no." Like those who say "I believe in God but not in priests." But it is the Church herself which brings Christ to us and which brings us to God. The Church is the great family of God's children. Of course, she also has human aspects. In those who make up the Church, pastors and faithful, there are shortcomings, imperfections and sins. The Pope has these too—and many of them; but what is beautiful is that when we realize we are sinners we encounter the mercy of God who always forgives. Never forget it: God always pardons and receives us into his love of forgiveness and mercy. Some people say that sin is an offense to God, but also an opportunity to humble oneself so as to realize that there is something else more beautiful: God's mercy.

GENERAL AUDIENCE, ST. PETER'S SQUARE
WEDNESDAY, MAY 29, 2013

Do I Pray for the Church?

Let us ask ourselves today: how much do I love the Church? Do I pray for her? Do I feel part of the family of the Church? What do I do to ensure that she is a community in which each one feels welcome and understood, feels the mercy and love of God who renews life? Faith is a gift and an act which concern us personally, but God calls us to live with our faith together, as a family, as Church.

GENERAL AUDIENCE, ST. PETER'S SQUARE
WEDNESDAY, MAY 29, 2013

A Powerful Sense of God's Mercy

In Christianity there is no contrast between sacred and profane.... There is a remarkable idea that struck me, on thinking about the legacy of St. Celestine V, who, like St. Francis of Assisi, had a really powerful sense of God's mercy, and of the fact that the mercy of God renews the world. Peter of Morrone, like Francis of Assisi, knew well the society of his time, with its great poverty. They were very close to the people. They had the same compassion Jesus had toward so many weary and oppressed people; but they did not limit themselves to offering good advice, or sympathetic consolation. First of all they chose a life that went against the current, they chose to entrust themselves to the Providence of the Father, not only as a personal ascesis, but as prophetic witnesses to a Paternity and to fraternity, which is the message of the Gospel of Jesus Christ. And it always strikes me that with their powerful compassion for the people, these Saints felt the need to give the people the greatest thing, the greatest wealth: the Father's mercy, forgiveness.

MEETING WITH ALL THE CITIZENS AND PROCLAMATION
OF THE CELESTINE JUBILEE YEAR
PIAZZA DELLA CATTEDRALE (ISERNIA)
SATURDAY, JULY 5, 2014

A Time for Renewal

[A Jubilee Year] is not an escape, not an avoidance of reality and of one's problems, it is the answer that comes from the Gospel: love as a force of purification, of integrity, a force of renewal of social relationships, a force of planning for a different economy, which places the person, work and family at the center rather than money and profit. We are all aware that this is not the way of the world; we are not dreamers, mistaken, nor do we want to create an out-of-this-world oasis. We believe rather that this is the good path for all, it is the path that truly brings us close to justice and peace. But we also know that we are sinners, that we are always tempted at first not to follow this path and to conform to the world's mentality, to the mentality of power, to the mentality of wealth. This is why we entrust ourselves to God's mercy, and we commit ourselves to carrying out with his grace the fruit of conversion and works of mercy. These two things: to convert oneself and perform works of mercy.

MEETING WITH ALL THE CITIZENS AND PROCLAMATION
OF THE CELESTINE JUBILEE YEAR
PIAZZA DELLA CATTEDRALE (ISERNIA)
SATURDAY, JULY 5, 2014

GOING OUTSIDE OUR OWN CONCERNS

The Church which "goes forth" is a community of missionary disciples who take the first step, who are involved and supportive, who bear fruit and rejoice. An evangelizing community knows that the Lord has taken the initiative, he has loved us first (cf. 1 Jn 4:19), and therefore we can move forward, boldly take the initiative, go out to others, seek those who have fallen away, stand at the crossroads and welcome the outcast. Such a community has an endless desire to show mercy, the fruit of its own experience of the power of the Father's infinite mercy. Let us try a little harder to take the first step and to become involved. Jesus washed the feet of his disciples. The Lord gets involved and he involves his own, as he kneels to wash their feet. He tells his disciples: "You will be blessed if you do this" (Jn 13:17). An evangelizing community gets involved by word and deed in people's daily lives; it bridges distances, it is willing to abase itself if necessary, and it embraces human life, touching the suffering flesh of Christ in others. Evangelizers thus take on the "smell of the sheep" and the sheep are willing to hear their voice.

EVANGELII GAUDIUM, 24

GOD NEVER TIRES OF FORGIVING US

Now is the time to say to Jesus: "Lord, I have let myself be deceived; in a thousand ways I have shunned your love, yet here I am once more, to renew my covenant with you. I need you. Save me once again, Lord, take me once more into your redeeming embrace." How good it feels to come back to him whenever we are lost! Let me say this once more: God never tires of forgiving us; we are the ones who tire of seeking his mercy. Christ, who told us to forgive one another "seventy times seven" (Mt 18:22) has given us his example: he has forgiven us seventy times seven. Time and time again he bears us on his shoulders. No one can strip us of the dignity bestowed upon us by this boundless and unfailing love. With a tenderness which never disappoints, but is always capable of restoring our joy, he makes it possible for us to lift up our heads and to start anew. Let us not flee from the resurrection of Jesus, let us never give up, come what will. May nothing inspire more than his life, which impels us onwards!

EVANGELII GAUDIUM, 3

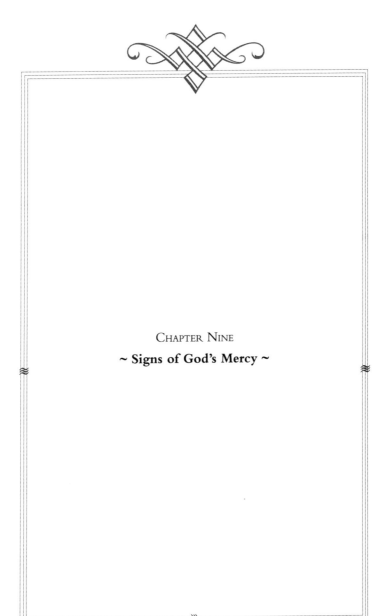

CHAPTER NINE

~ **Signs of God's Mercy** ~

Drawn into God's Mercy

When Jesus received the baptism of repentance from John the Baptist, showing solidarity with the repentant people—He without sin and with no need for conversion—God the Father made his voice heard from heaven: "This is my beloved Son, with whom I am well pleased" (v. 17). Jesus receives approval from the heavenly Father, who sent him precisely that he might accept to share our condition, our poverty. Sharing is the true way to love. Jesus does not dissociate himself from us, he considers us brothers and sisters and he shares with us. And so he makes us sons and daughters, together with him, of God the Father. This is the revelation and source of true love. And this is the great time of mercy!

ANGELUS, ST. PETER'S SQUARE
SUNDAY, JANUARY 12, 2014

The Path Traced Out by Our Baptism

Does it not seem to you that in our own time extra fraternal sharing and love is needed? Does it not seem to you that we all need extra charity? Not the sort that is content with extemporaneous help which does not involve or stake anything, but that charity that shares, that takes on the hardship and suffering of a brother. What flavor life acquires when we allow ourselves to be inundated by God's love! Let us ask the Holy Virgin to support us by her intercession in our commitment to follow Christ on the way of faith and charity, the path traced out by our Baptism.

ANGELUS, ST. PETER'S SQUARE
SUNDAY, JANUARY 12, 2014

Lord, Have Mercy

At the beginning of Mass, every time, we are called before the Lord to recognize that we are sinners, expressing through words and gestures sincere repentance of the heart. And we say: "Have mercy on me, Lord. I am a sinner! I confess to Almighty God my sins." And we don't say: "Lord, have mercy on this man who is beside me, or this woman, who are sinners." No! "Have mercy on me!" We are all sinners and in need of the Lord's forgiveness. It is the Holy Spirit who speaks to our spirit and makes us recognize our faults in light of the Word of Jesus. And Jesus himself invites us all, saints and sinners, to his table, gathering us from the crossroads, from diverse situations of life (cf. Mt 22:9–10).

ANGELUS, ST. PETER'S SQUARE
SUNDAY, SEPTEMBER 7, 2014

Opening Wide the Doors

Among the conditions in common among those participating in the Eucharistic celebration, two are fundamental in order to go to Mass correctly: we are all sinners and God grants his mercy to all. These are the two conditions which open wide the doors that we might enter Mass properly.

ANGELUS, ST. PETER'S SQUARE
SUNDAY, SEPTEMBER 7, 2014

Don't Put Obstacles in the Path

The confessional must not be a torture chamber but rather an encounter with the Lord's mercy which spurs us on to do our best. A small step, in the midst of great human limitations, can be more pleasing to God than a life which appears outwardly in order but moves through the day without confronting great difficulties. Everyone needs to be touched by the comfort and attraction of God's saving love, which is mysteriously at work in each person, above and beyond their faults and failings.

EVANGELII GAUDIUM, 44

THE VERY LIFE OF GOD

The love of Jesus Christ lasts forever, it has no end because it is the very life of God. This love conquers sin and gives the strength to rise and begin again, for through forgiveness the heart is renewed and rejuvenated. We all know it: our Father never tires of loving and his eyes never grow weary of watching the road to his home to see if the son who left and was lost is returning. We can speak of God's hope: our Father expects us always, he doesn't just leave the door open to us, but he awaits us. He is engaged in the waiting for his children. And this Father also does not tire of loving the other son who, though staying at home with him the whole time, does not share in his mercy, in his compassion. God is not only at the origin of love, but in Jesus Christ he calls us to imitate his own way of loving: "as I have loved you, that you also love one another" (Jn 13:34). To the extent to which Christians live this love, they become credible disciples of Christ to the world. Love cannot bear being locked up in itself. By its nature it is open, it spreads and bears fruit, it always kindles new love.

COMMUNAL RECONCILIATION SERVICE,
VATICAN BASILICA
FRIDAY, MARCH 28, 2014

Communicate the Joy of Forgiveness

To the many you will meet, you can communicate the joy of receiving the forgiveness of the Father and of rediscovering full friendship with him. And you will tell them that our Father expects us, our Father forgives us, and furthermore that he rejoices. If you go to him with your whole life, even with the many sins, instead of reproaching you, he will rejoice: this is our Father. This you must say, say it to many people, today. Whoever experiences divine mercy, is impelled to be an architect of mercy among the least and the poor. In these "littlest brothers" Jesus awaits us (cf. Mt 25:40); let us receive mercy and let us give mercy! Let us go to the encounter and let us celebrate Easter in the joy of God!

COMMUNAL RECONCILIATION SERVICE,
VATICAN BASILICA
FRIDAY, MARCH 28, 2014

Shaped by God's Grace

As the Apostle Paul reminds us, God never ceases to show the richness of His mercy throughout the ages. The transformation of the heart that leads us to confess our sins is "God's gift," it is "His work" (cf. Eph 2:8–10). To be touched with tenderness by His hand and shaped by His grace allows us, therefore, to approach the priest without fear for our sins, but with the certainty of being welcomed by him in the name of God, and understood notwithstanding our miseries. Coming out of the confessional, we will feel God's strength, which restores life and returns the enthusiasm of faith.

24 HOURS FOR THE LORD, ST. PETER'S BASILICA
FRIDAY, MARCH 13, 2015

The Grandeur of God's Mercy

Let us place the Sacrament of Reconciliation at the center once more in such a way that it will enable people to touch the grandeur of God's mercy with their own hands. For every penitent, it will be a source of true interior peace. I will never tire of insisting that confessors be authentic signs of the Father's mercy. We do not become good confessors automatically. We become good confessors when, above all, we allow ourselves to be penitents in search of his mercy.

MISERICORDIAE VULTUS, BULL OF INDICTION OF THE
EXTRAORDINARY JUBILEE YEAR OF MERCY, 17

THE CONSTANCY OF DIVINE LOVE

Let us never forget that to be confessors means to participate in the very mission of Jesus to be a concrete sign of the constancy of divine love that pardons and saves. We priests have received the gift of the Holy Spirit for the forgiveness of sins, and we are responsible for this. None of us wields power over this Sacrament; rather, we are faithful servants of God's mercy through it. Every confessor must accept the faithful as the father in the parable of the prodigal son: a father who runs out to meet his son despite the fact that he has squandered away his inheritance. Confessors are called to embrace the repentant son who comes back home and to express the joy of having him back again. Let us never tire of also going out to the other son who stands outside, incapable of rejoicing, in order to explain to him that his judgment is severe and unjust and meaningless in light of the father's boundless mercy.

MISERICORDIAE VULTUS, BULL OF INDICTION OF THE
EXTRAORDINARY JUBILEE YEAR OF MERCY, 17

Marriage Is a Symbol of Life

The love of Christ, which has blessed and sanctified the union of husband and wife, is able to sustain their love and to renew it when, humanly speaking, it becomes lost, wounded or worn out. The love of Christ can restore to spouses the joy of journeying together. The path is not always a smooth one, free of disagreements, otherwise it would not be human. It is a demanding journey, at times difficult, and at times turbulent, but such is life! It is normal for husband and wife to argue: it's normal. It always happens. But my advice is this: never let the day end without having first made peace. Never! A small gesture is sufficient. Thus the journey may continue. Marriage is a symbol of life, real life: it is not "fiction"! It is the Sacrament of the love of Christ and the Church, a love which finds its proof and guarantee in the Cross. There will be crosses! But the Lord is always there to help us move forward. May the Lord bless you!

HOLY MASS WITH THE RITE OF MARRIAGE,
ST. PETER'S SQUARE
SUNDAY, SEPTEMBER 14, 2014

BRINGING GOD'S MERCY TO THE SICK

There is a biblical icon that expresses, in all its depths, the mystery that shines through the Anointing of the Sick: it is the parable of the "Good Samaritan" contained in the Gospel of Luke (10:30–35). Each time that we celebrate this Sacrament, the Lord Jesus, in the person of the priest, comes close to the one who suffers and is seriously ill or elderly. The parable says that the Good Samaritan takes care of the suffering man by pouring oil and wine on his wounds. Oil makes us think of that which is blessed by the Bishop each year at the Holy Thursday Chrism Mass, precisely in view of the Anointing of the Sick. Wine, however, is a sign of Christ's love and grace, which flow from the gift of his life for us and are expressed in all their richness in the sacramental life of the Church. Finally, the suffering person is entrusted to an innkeeper, so that he might continue to care for him, sparing no expense. Now, who is this innkeeper? It is the Church, the Christian community—it is us—to whom each day the Lord entrusts those who are afflicted in body and spirit, so that we might lavish all of his mercy and salvation upon them without measure.

GENERAL AUDIENCE, ST. PETER'S SQUARE
WEDNESDAY, FEBRUARY 26, 2014

THE LORD HEALS THE SICK

The priest and those who are present during the Anointing of the Sick, in fact, represent the entire Christian community that as one body huddles around the one who suffers and his family, nurturing their faith and hope, and supporting them through their prayers and fraternal warmth. But the greatest comfort comes from the fact that it is the Lord Jesus himself who makes himself present in the Sacrament, who takes us by the hand, who caresses us as he did with the sick, and who reminds us that we already belong to him and that nothing—not even evil and death—can ever separate us from him.

GENERAL AUDIENCE, ST. PETER'S SQUARE
WEDNESDAY, FEBRUARY 26, 2014

CHAPTER TEN

~Vocation: Called to Show God's Mercy ~

KNOWING WE ARE LOVED BY GOD

The firm conviction of being loved by God is at the center of your vocation: to be for others a tangible sign of the presence of God's Kingdom, a foretaste of the eternal joys of heaven. Only if our witness is joyful will we attract men and women to Christ. And this joy is a gift which is nourished by a life of prayer, meditation on the word of God, the celebration of the sacraments and life in community, which is very important. When these are lacking, weaknesses and difficulties will emerge to dampen the joy we knew so well at the beginning of our journey.

MEETING WITH THE RELIGIOUS COMMUNITIES OF
KOREA, TRAINING CENTER "SCHOOL OF LOVE"
(KKOTTONGNAE)
SATURDAY, AUGUST 16, 2014

COMMUNITY: A TRAINING GROUND FOR THE HEART

For you, as men and women consecrated to God, this joy is rooted in the mystery of the Father's mercy revealed in Christ's sacrifice on the cross. Whether the charism of your Institute is directed more to contemplation or to the active life, you are challenged to become "experts" in divine mercy precisely through your life in community. From experience I know that community life is not always easy, but it is a providential training ground for the heart. It is unrealistic not to expect conflicts; misunderstandings will arise and they must be faced. Despite such difficulties, it is in community life that we are called to grow in mercy, forbearance and perfect charity.

MEETING WITH THE RELIGIOUS COMMUNITIES OF
KOREA, TRAINING CENTER "SCHOOL OF LOVE"
(KKOTTONGNAE)
SATURDAY, AUGUST 16, 2014

WITNESS TO GOD'S LOVE

The experience of God's mercy, nourished by prayer and community, must shape all that you are, all that you do. Your chastity, poverty and obedience will be a joyful witness to God's love in the measure that you stand firmly on the rock of his mercy. That is the rock. This is certainly the case with religious obedience. Mature and generous obedience requires that you cling in prayer to Christ who, taking the form of a servant, learned obedience through what he suffered (cf. *Perfectae Caritatis,* 14). There are no shortcuts: God desires our hearts completely and this means we have to "let go" and "go out" of ourselves more and more.

MEETING WITH THE RELIGIOUS COMMUNITIES OF
KOREA, TRAINING CENTER "SCHOOL OF LOVE"
(KKOTTONGNAE)
SATURDAY, AUGUST 16, 2014

An Interior Attitude of Compassion

Where was Jesus most often, where he could most easily be found? On the road. He might have seemed to be homeless, because he was always on the road. Jesus' life was on the road. He especially invites us to grasp the depths of his heart, what he feels for the crowds, for the people he encounters: that interior attitude of "compassion"; seeing the crowds, he felt compassion for them. For he saw the people were "harassed and helpless, like sheep without a shepherd." We have heard these words so many times that perhaps they do not strike us powerfully. But they are powerful! A little like the many people whom you meet today on the streets of your own neighborhoods.... Then the horizon broadens, and we see that these towns and villages are not only Rome and Italy; they are the world... and those helpless crowds are the peoples of many nations who are suffering through even more difficult situations....

ADDRESS TO THE PARISH PRIESTS
OF THE DIOCESE OF ROME, PAUL VI HALL
THURSDAY, MARCH 6, 2014

Treating the Wounded

The priest is called to learn this, to have a heart that is moved. Priests who are—allow me to say the word—"aseptic," those "from the laboratory," all clean and tidy, do not help the Church. Today we can think of the Church as a "field hospital." Excuse me but I repeat it, because this is how I see it, how I feel it is: a "field hospital." Wounds need to be treated, so many wounds! So many wounds! There are so many people who are wounded by material problems, by scandals, also in the Church.... People wounded by the world's illusions.... We priests must be there, close to these people. Mercy first means treating the wounds. When someone is wounded, he needs this immediately, not tests such as the level of cholesterol and one's glycemic index.... But there's a wound, treat the wound, and then we can look at the results of the tests. Then specialized treatments can be done, but first we need to treat the open wounds. I think this is what is most important at this time.

ADDRESS TO THE PARISH PRIESTS
OF THE DIOCESE OF ROME, PAUL VI HALL
THURSDAY, MARCH 6, 2014

PERCEIVING THE HIDDEN WOUNDS

And there are also hidden wounds, because there are people who distance themselves in order to avoid showing their wounds closer.... The custom comes to mind, in the Mosaic Law, of the lepers in Jesus' time, who were always kept at a distance in order not to spread the contagion.... There are people who distance themselves through shame, through shame, so as not to let their wounds be seen.... And perhaps they distance themselves with some bitterness against the Church, but deep down inside there is a wound.... And you, dear brothers—I ask you—do you know the wounds of your parishioners? Do you perceive them? Are you close to them? It's the only question....

ADDRESS TO THE PARISH PRIESTS
OF THE DIOCESE OF ROME, PAUL VI HALL
THURSDAY, MARCH 6, 2014

HAVING THE HEART OF CHRIST

True mercy takes the person into one's care, listens to him attentively, approaches the situation with respect and truth, and accompanies him on the journey of reconciliation. And this is demanding, yes, certainly. The truly merciful priest behaves like the Good Samaritan...but why does he do it? Because his heart is capable of having compassion, it is the heart of Christ!

ADDRESS TO THE PARISH PRIESTS
OF THE DIOCESE OF ROME, PAUL VI HALL
THURSDAY, MARCH 6, 2014

THE DOORS OF MERCY

I want to pause to ask you, for the love of Jesus Christ: never tire of being merciful! Please! Have the ability to forgive that the Lord had, who came not to condemn but to forgive! Be greatly merciful! And if you have scruples about being too "forgiving," think of that holy priest about whom I have told you, who went before the Tabernacle and said: "Lord, pardon me if I have forgiven too much, but it is you who have set me a bad example!" And I tell you, truly: it grieves me when I come across people who no longer confess because they have been beaten and scolded. They have felt as though the church doors were being closed in their faces! Please, do not do this: mercy, mercy! The Good Shepherd enters through the door, and the doors of mercy are the wounds of the Lord: if you do not enter into your ministry through the Lord's wounds, you will not be good shepherds.

HOLY MASS WITH PRIESTLY ORDINATIONS,
VATICAN BASILICA
FOURTH SUNDAY OF EASTER, MAY 11, 2014

THE WAY OF HOLINESS IS MERCY

Jesus did not come to teach us good manners, how to behave well at the table! To do that, he would not have had to come down from heaven and die on the Cross. Christ came to save us, to show us the way, the only way out of the quicksand of sin, and this way of holiness is mercy, that mercy which he has shown, and daily continues to show, to us. To be a saint is not a luxury. It is necessary for the salvation of the world. This is what the Lord is asking of us.

HOLY MASS WITH THE NEW CARDINALS,
VATICAN BASILICA
SUNDAY, FEBRUARY 23, 2014

CHAPTER ELEVEN

~ Ecumenism: Going Outside the Doors ~

An Inexhaustible Richness

There is an aspect of mercy that goes beyond the confines of the Church. It relates us to Judaism and Islam, both of which consider mercy to be one of God's most important attributes. Israel was the first to receive this revelation which continues in history as the source of an inexhaustible richness meant to be shared with all mankind. As we have seen, the pages of the Old Testament are steeped in mercy, because they narrate the works that the Lord performed in favor of his people at the most trying moments of their history.

MISERICORDIAE VULTUS, BULL OF INDICTION OF THE
EXTRAORDINARY JUBILEE YEAR OF MERCY, 23

Merciful and Kind

Among the privileged names that Islam attributes to the Creator are "Merciful and Kind." This invocation is often on the lips of faithful Muslims who feel themselves accompanied and sustained by mercy in their daily weakness. They too believe that no one can place a limit on divine mercy because its doors are always open.

MISERICORDIAE VULTUS, BULL OF INDICTION OF THE
EXTRAORDINARY JUBILEE YEAR OF MERCY, 23

Open to Dialogue

I trust that this Jubilee year celebrating the mercy of God will foster an encounter with these religions and with other noble religious traditions; may it open us to even more fervent dialogue so that we might know and understand one another better; may it eliminate every form of closed-mindedness and disrespect, and drive out every form of violence and discrimination.

MISERICORDIAE VULTUS, BULL OF INDICTION OF THE EXTRAORDINARY JUBILEE YEAR OF MERCY, 23

The Tragedy of Division

Clearly we cannot deny the divisions which continue to exist among us, the disciples of Jesus: this sacred place makes us even more painfully aware of how tragic they are. And yet, fifty years after the embrace of those two venerable Fathers, we realize with gratitude and renewed amazement how it was possible, at the prompting of the Holy Spirit, to take truly significant steps towards unity. We know that much distance still needs to be travelled before we attain that fullness of communion which can also be expressed by sharing the same Eucharistic table, something we ardently desire; yet our disagreements must not frighten us and paralyze our progress.

BASILICA OF THE HOLY SEPULCHRE (JERUSALEM)
SUNDAY, MAY 25, 2014

THE CHURCH'S VOCATION TO UNITY

We need to believe that, just as the stone before the tomb was cast aside, so too every obstacle to our full communion will also be removed. This will be a grace of resurrection, of which we can have a foretaste even today. Every time we ask forgiveness of one another for our sins against other Christians and every time we find the courage to grant and receive such forgiveness, we experience the resurrection! Every time we put behind us our longstanding prejudices and find the courage to build new fraternal relationships, we confess that Christ is truly risen! Every time we reflect on the future of the Church in the light of her vocation to unity, the dawn of Easter breaks forth! Here I reiterate the hope already expressed by my predecessors for a continued dialogue with all our brothers and sisters in Christ, aimed at finding a means of exercising the specific ministry of the Bishop of Rome which, in fidelity to his mission, can be open to a new situation and can be, in the present context, a service of love and of communion acknowledged by all (cf. John Paul II, *Ut Unum Sint,* 95–96).

BASILICA OF THE HOLY SEPULCHRE (JERUSALEM)
SUNDAY, MAY 25, 2014

SUFFERING TOGETHER SIDE BY SIDE

Standing as pilgrims in these holy places, we also remember in our prayers the entire Middle East, so frequently and lamentably marked by acts of violence and conflict. Nor do we forget in our prayers the many other men and women who in various parts of our world are suffering from war, poverty and hunger, as well as the many Christians who are persecuted for their faith in the risen Lord. When Christians of different confessions suffer together, side by side, and assist one another with fraternal charity, there is born an ecumenism of suffering, an ecumenism of blood, which proves particularly powerful not only for those situations in which it occurs, but also, by virtue of the communion of the saints, for the whole Church as well. Those who kill, persecute Christians out of hatred, do not ask if they are Orthodox or Catholics: they are Christians. The blood of Christians is the same.

BASILICA OF THE HOLY SEPULCHRE (JERUSALEM)
SUNDAY, MAY 25, 2014

OPEN TO THE SPIRIT OF UNITY

Let us put aside the misgivings we have inherited from the past and open our hearts to the working of the Holy Spirit, the Spirit of love (cf. Rom 5:5), in order to hasten together towards that blessed day when our full communion will be restored. In making this journey, we feel ourselves sustained by the prayer which Jesus himself, in this city, on the eve of his passion, death and resurrection, offered to the Father for his disciples. It is a prayer which we ourselves in humility never tire to make our own: "that they may all be one...that the world may believe" (Jn 17:21). And when disunity makes us pessimistic, distrusting, fearful, let us all commend ourselves to the protection of the Holy Mother of God. When there is spiritual turmoil in the Christian soul, it is only by seeking refuge under her mantle that we can find peace. May the Holy Mother of God help us on this journey.

BASILICA OF THE HOLY SEPULCHRE (JERUSALEM)
SUNDAY, MAY 25, 2014

The Sin of Division

In the face of all of this, we must make a serious examination of conscience. In a Christian community, division is one of the gravest sins, because it makes it a sign not of God's work, but of the devil's work, who is by definition the one who separates, who destroys relationships, who insinuates prejudice.... Division in a Christian community, whether in a school, a parish, or an association, it is a very grave sin, because it is the work of the Devil. God, instead wants us to develop the capacity to welcome, to forgive and to love each other, to be ever more like Him, who is communion and love. The Church's holiness consists in this: in recognizing herself in God's image, showered with his mercy and his grace.

GENERAL AUDIENCE, ST. PETER'S SQUARE
WEDNESDAY, AUGUST 27, 2014

The World Suffocates without Dialogue

More prayer and more dialogue are needed: they're necessary. The world suffocates without dialogue. Dialogue is only possible starting from true identity. I cannot pretend to have a different identity in order to dialogue. No, it isn't possible to dialogue in this way. This is my identity and I dialogue because I'm a person, because I'm a man or a woman; and man and woman have the opportunity to dialogue without negotiating their identity. The world suffocates without dialogue: for this you also make your contribution, in order to promote friendship among religions.

ADDRESS TO THE SANT'EGIDIO COMMUNITY, BASILICA
OF "SANTA MARIA IN TRASTEVERE"
SUNDAY, JUNE 15, 2014

CULTIVATING FRIENDSHIP

Go forth on this path: prayer, the poor and peace. And as you walk this path, you help compassion grow in the heart of society—which is the true revolution, that of compassion and tenderness—to cultivate friendship in place of the ghosts of animosity and indifference.

ADDRESS TO THE SANT'EGIDIO COMMUNITY, BASILICA OF "SANTA MARIA IN TRASTEVERE" SUNDAY, JUNE 15, 2014

CHAPTER TWELVE

~ The Works of Mercy: Bringing Everyone Inside ~

Opening Our Hearts

In this Holy Year, we look forward to the experience
of opening our hearts to those living on the outermost
fringes of society: fringes which modern society itself
creates. How many uncertain and painful situations there
are in the world today! How many are the wounds borne
by the flesh of those who have no voice because their
cry is muffled and drowned out by the indifference of the
rich! During this Jubilee, the Church will be called even
more to heal these wounds, to assuage them with the oil of
consolation, to bind them with mercy and cure them with
solidarity and vigilant care.

MISERICORDIAE VULTUS, BULL OF INDICTION OF THE
EXTRAORDINARY JUBILEE YEAR OF MERCY, 15

Avoiding Cynicism and Indifference

Let us not fall into humiliating indifference or a monotonous routine that prevents us from discovering what is new! Let us ward off destructive cynicism! Let us open our eyes and see the misery of the world, the wounds of our brothers and sisters who are denied their dignity, and let us recognize that we are compelled to heed their cry for help! May we reach out to them and support them so they can feel the warmth of our presence, our friendship, and our fraternity! May their cry become our own, and together may we break down the barriers of indifference that too often reign supreme and mask our hypocrisy and egoism!

MISERICORDIAE VULTUS, BULL OF INDICTION OF THE EXTRAORDINARY JUBILEE YEAR OF MERCY, 15

How Will God Judge Us?

We cannot escape the Lord's words to us, and they will serve as the criteria upon which we will be judged: whether we have fed the hungry and given drink to the thirsty, welcomed the stranger and clothed the naked, or spent time with the sick and those in prison (cf. Mt 25:31–45). Moreover, we will be asked if we have helped others to escape the doubt that causes them to fall into despair and which is often a source of loneliness; if we have helped to overcome the ignorance in which millions of people live, especially children deprived of the necessary means to free them from the bonds of poverty; if we have been close to the lonely and afflicted; if we have forgiven those who have offended us and have rejected all forms of anger and hate that lead to violence; if we have had the kind of patience God shows, who is so patient with us; and if we have commended our brothers and sisters to the Lord in prayer. In each of these "little ones," Christ himself is present. His flesh becomes visible in the flesh of the tortured, the crushed, the scourged, the malnourished, and the exiled…to be acknowledged, touched, and cared for by us. Let us not forget the words of Saint John of the Cross: "as we prepare to leave this life, we will be judged on the basis of love" (St. John of the Cross, *Words of Light and Love,* 57).

MISERICORDIAE VULTUS, BULL OF INDICTION OF THE
EXTRAORDINARY JUBILEE YEAR OF MERCY, 15

The Heart of the Gospel

It is my burning desire that, during this Jubilee, the Christian people may reflect on the corporal and spiritual works of mercy. It will be a way to reawaken our conscience, too often grown dull in the face of poverty. And let us enter more deeply into the heart of the Gospel where the poor have a special experience of God's mercy. Jesus introduces us to these works of mercy in his preaching so that we can know whether or not we are living as his disciples. Let us rediscover these corporal works of mercy: to feed the hungry, give drink to the thirsty, clothe the naked, welcome the stranger, heal the sick, visit the imprisoned, and bury the dead. And let us not forget the spiritual works of mercy: to counsel the doubtful, instruct the ignorant, admonish sinners, comfort the afflicted, forgive offenses, bear patiently those who do us ill, and pray for the living and the dead.

MISERICORDIAE VULTUS, BULL OF INDICTION OF THE
EXTRAORDINARY JUBILEE YEAR OF MERCY, 15

Remembering the Dead

Yesterday and today, many have been visiting cemeteries, which, as the word itself implies, is the "place of rest," as we wait for the final awakening. It is lovely to think that it will be Jesus himself to awaken us. Jesus himself revealed that the death of the body is like a sleep from which He awakens us. With this faith we pause—even spiritually—at the graves of our loved ones, of those who loved us and did us good. But today we are called to remember everyone, even those whom no one remembers. We remember the victims of war and violence; the many "little ones" of the world, crushed by hunger and poverty; we remember the anonymous who rest in the communal ossuary. We remember our brothers and sisters killed because they were Christian; and those who sacrificed their lives to serve others. We especially entrust to the Lord, those who have left us during the past year.

ANGELUS, ST. PETER'S SQUARE
SUNDAY, NOVEMBER 2, 2014

Sharing in the Lord's Work

The work of Jesus is, precisely, a work of mercy, a work of forgiveness and of love! Jesus is so full of mercy! And this universal pardon, this mercy, passes through the Cross. Jesus, however, does not want to do this work alone: he wants to involve us too in the mission that the Father entrusted to him. After the Resurrection he was to say to his disciples: "As the Father has sent me, even so I send you"…if you forgive the sins of any, they are forgiven" (Jn 20:21–22). Jesus' disciple renounces all his possessions because in Jesus he has found the greatest Good in which every other good receives its full value and meaning: family ties, other relationships, work, cultural and economic goods and so forth.... The Christian detaches him or herself from all things and rediscovers all things in the logic of the Gospel, the logic of love and of service.

ANGELUS, ST. PETER'S SQUARE
SUNDAY, SEPTEMBER 8, 2013

Simple Hospitality

The rule of hospitality has always been sacred in the simplest Christian families: there is always a plate and a bed for the one in need. A mother once told me that she wanted to teach this to her children and she told them to help and feed those who were hungry. One day at lunch there came a knock at the door: there was a man who asked for something to eat. And the mama told him: "Wait a moment." She went back inside and told her children: "There's a man there asking for something to eat, what can we do?" "Let's give him something, Mama, let's give him something!" Each of them had a beefsteak and fried potatoes on their plate. "Very well, let's take half from each of you, and we'll give him half." And this is how this mom taught her children to give food from their own plate. This is a fine example that really helped me. This is what Mother Church teaches us.

GENERAL AUDIENCE, ST. PETER'S SQUARE
WEDNESDAY, SEPTEMBER 10, 2014

Teaching by Example

The Church conducts herself like Jesus. She does not teach theoretical lessons on love, on mercy. She does not spread to the world a philosophy, a way of wisdom.... Of course, Christianity is also all of this, but as an effect, by reflex. Mother Church, like Jesus, teaches by example, and the words serve to illuminate the meaning of her actions. Mother Church teaches us to give food and drink to those who are hungry and thirsty, to clothe those who are naked. And how does she do this? She does it through the example of so many saints, men and women, who did this in an exemplary fashion; but she does it also through the example of so many dads and mamas, who teach their children that what we have extra is for those who lack the basic necessities. It is important to know this.

GENERAL AUDIENCE, ST. PETER'S SQUARE
WEDNESDAY, SEPTEMBER 10, 2014

CARE FOR PRISONERS

Mother Church teaches us to be close to those who are in prison. "But no Father, this is dangerous, those are bad people." But each of us is capable.... Listen carefully to this: each of us is capable of doing the same thing that that man or that woman in prison did. All of us have the capacity to sin and to do the same, to make mistakes in life. They are no worse than you and me! Mercy overcomes every wall, every barrier, and leads you to always seek the face of the man, of the person. And it is mercy which changes the heart and the life, which can regenerate a person and allow him or her to integrate into society in a new way.

GENERAL AUDIENCE, ST. PETER'S SQUARE
WEDNESDAY, SEPTEMBER 10, 2014

No One Should Die Alone

Mother Church teaches us to be close to those who are neglected and die alone. Mercy gives peace to those who pass away and those who remain, allowing them to feel that God is greater than death, and that abiding in Him even the last parting is a "see you again".... The blessed Teresa understood this well! They told her: "Mother, this is a waste of time!" She found people dying on the street, people whose bodies were being eaten by mice on the street, and she took them home so they could die clean, calm, touched gently, in peace. She gave them a "see you again," to all of them.... And so many men and women like her have done this. And they are awaiting them, there [pointing to heaven], at the gate, to open the gate of Heaven to them. Help people die serenely, in peace.

GENERAL AUDIENCE, ST. PETER'S SQUARE
WEDNESDAY, SEPTEMBER 10, 2014

"It Is Not Enough to Look, We Must Follow!"
Jesus did not come into the world to be in a parade.... He did not come for this. Jesus is the path and a path is for walking and following. We cannot follow Jesus on the path of love unless we first love others, unless we force ourselves to work together, to understand each other and to forgive each another, recognizing our own limits and mistakes. We must do works of mercy and with mercy! Putting our heart in them. Works of charity with love, with tenderness and always with humility! For the Good Shepherd what is far, what is on the margins, what is lost and unappreciated is the object of greater care and the Church cannot but make her own this special love and attention. The first in the Church are those who are the most in need, humanly, spiritually, materially, the neediest.

MEETING WITH THE POOR AND PRISON INMATES,
CATHEDRAL OF CAGLIARI
SUNDAY, SEPTEMBER 22, 2013

Our Goods Are Meant to Be Used, Not Hoarded

Jesus does not ask us to store his grace in a safe! Jesus does not ask us for this, but He wants us to use it to benefit others. All the goods that we have received are to give to others, and thus they increase, as if He were to tell us: "Here is my mercy, my tenderness, my forgiveness: take them and make ample use of them." And what have we done with them? Whom have we "infected" with our faith? How many people have we encouraged with our hope? How much love have we shared with our neighbor? These are questions that will do us good to ask ourselves. Any environment, even the furthest and most impractical, can become a place where our talents can bear fruit. There are no situations or places precluded from the Christian presence and witness. The witness which Jesus asks of us is not closed, but is open, it is in our hands.

ANGELUS, ST. PETER'S SQUARE
SUNDAY, NOVEMBER 16, 2014

OPENING OUR HEARTS TO THE WRETCHED

All of your service derives meaning and form from this word: "*misericordia*" [mercy], a Latin word whose etymological meaning is "*miseris cor dare,*" to "give the heart to the wretched," those in need, those who are suffering. That is what Jesus did: he opened his heart to the wretchedness of man. From the Gospel narratives we are able to understand the closeness, the goodness, the tenderness with which Jesus drew in the suffering people and consoled them, comforted them, and often healed them. By our Teacher's example, we too are called to draw near, to share the conditions of the people we meet. It is necessary that our words, our actions, our attitudes express solidarity, the will to not remain alien to the pain of others, and do this with fraternal warmth and without falling into some form of paternalism.

ADDRESS TO THE NATIONAL CONFEDERATION
OF THE "MISERICORDIE" OF ITALY,
ST. PETER'S SQUARE
SATURDAY, JUNE 14, 2014

Work, Not Words

We've heard many words! What's needed is work, Christian testimony, going to the suffering, getting close to them as Jesus did. Let us imitate Jesus: He goes to the streets, not planning for the poor or the sick or disabled people that he crosses along the way; but with the first one he encounters, he stops, becoming a presence of care, a sign of the closeness of God who is goodness, providence and love. The activity of your associations is inspired by the Seven Corporal Works of Mercy, which I would like to recall, because it will be good to hear them again: to feed the hungry; to give drink to the thirsty; to clothe the naked; to harbor the homeless; to visit the sick; to visit the imprisoned; to bury the dead. I encourage you to carry on your work with joy and to model it after Christ's, allowing all who suffer to encounter you and count on you in time of need.

ADDRESS TO THE NATIONAL CONFEDERATION
OF THE "MISERICORDIE" OF ITALY,
ST. PETER'S SQUARE
SATURDAY, JUNE 14, 2014

A Life Plan

This is the life plan that Jesus proposes to us. A plan that is really simple but really difficult at the same time. And if we want something more, Jesus gives us even further instructions. In particular, he noted, is the protocol on which we will be judged, found in the Gospel of Matthew: "I was hungry and you gave me food; I was thirsty and you gave me drink; I was sick and you visited me; I was in prison and you came to me." This is the path to live the Christian life in a holy way. The saints did nothing other than live the beatitudes and that protocol of final judgment. They are few words, simple words, but practical for everyone, because Christianity is a practical religion, to practice, to do, not to simply think about.

MORNING MEDITATION IN THE CHAPEL OF THE
DOMUS SANCTAE MARTHAE
MONDAY, JUNE 9, 2014

About the Author

Pope Francis, formerly Cardinal Jorge Mario Bergoglio, S.J., served the Jesuits as novice master, lecturer, provincial, confessor, and spiritual director before Pope John Paul II named him Archbishop of Buenos Aires. He was elected to the papacy on March 13, 2013. He is the first pope from the Americas and the first pope to choose the name Francis, in honor of St. Francis of Assisi.

~ ~ ~

About the Editor

Diane M. Houdek is digital editor at Franciscan Media and the author of *Lent with St. Francis, Advent with St. Francis,* and *Pope Francis and Our Call to Joy.*